THE RYDER CUP 1965

HENRY LONGHURST & GEOFFREY COUSINS

THE RYDER CUP 1965

STANLEY PAUL · LONDON

STANLEY PAUL & CO LTD
178–202 Great Portland Street, London W1

 AN IMPRINT OF THE HUTCHINSON GROUP

London Melbourne Sydney
Auckland Bombay Toronto
Johannesburg New York

★

First published 1965

*This book has been set in Baskerville, printed in Great Britain
on Antique Wove paper by Anchor Press, and
bound by Wm. Brendon, both of Tiptree, Essex*

Contents

Acknowledgements

The authors are indebted to the publishers of
the 1965 Ryder Cup Programme for permission
to use some of their statistics contained therein.

Messrs. Gallaher Ltd. (makers of Senior
Service Cigarettes), on whose authority and
with whose support this record of the 1965
Ryder Cup Match has been produced, were
organisers of the 'Golf Village', first introduced
in the Senior Service Tournament at Dalmahoy;
and many Senior Service promotion ideas
were included in the set-up for the 1965 Ryder
Cup Match.

1 Highlights of the Past

As seen by
HENRY LONGHURST

THE Ryder Cup match which I should most dearly like to have seen was not a Ryder Cup match at all. It was the unofficial match at Wentworth in 1926, won incidentally by the British with the almost unbelievable score of 13 matches to 1, which led to Samuel Ryder presenting his Cup. I was a boy at school at the time but already in exhibition matches I had seen the two great British giants perform and one of them had become, and in many ways remains, my golfing hero. This was Abe Mitchell, and I still declare that if, blindfold, I could hear a dozen of the great players of today and yesterday driving a golf ball, I could tell you which one was Mitchell. The other was George Duncan. Their opponents throughout the day were two equally redoubtable golfers: Jim Barnes, the lanky, sardonic Cornishman long settled in America, a past open champion of that country and now at this moment British open champion, and the one and only Walter Hagen, also winner of the Open on both sides of the water. Hagen may on the surface have taken life light-heartedly but neither of these characters underneath their differing exteriors cared to be beaten. I should, of course, have run round with the four of them all day, sticking to the pair of them in the foursomes and alternating frantically between the two matches in the singles. I should have had to hurry too, for in the foursomes Mitchell and Duncan beat the Americans by 9 and 8 and on the next day Mitchell beat Barnes by 8 and 7, while Duncan beat Hagen by 6 and 5.

I did not see the first match for the Ryder Cup, which was played at Worcester, Mass., though when the British scored 1 point in the foursomes and $1\frac{1}{2}$ in the singles it seemed to set the pattern for future matches in America for a long time. The first home match for the Cup was played at Moortown, Leeds, in 1929, and part of this I did see. Three of us who were in the Cambridge University team at the time climbed out of college at about four in the morning and arrived at Leeds five or six hours later. All the giants were there— Hagen and Sarazen, Duncan and Mitchell again, Compston, Charles and Ernest Whitcombe, and an already publicised new-comer, T. H. Cotton. Duncan, craftily forecasting where Hagen

would play himself in the singles and anxious to prove that his
previous win was no fluke, flashed his way round Moortown—he
was undoubtedly the quickest great player of all time—to beat his
man by 10 and 8. The three of us became separated early on, as
golfing spectators always do, it being really a one man job, but
soon we found ourselves following the same match, with eyes for but
a single man. He was tall and slim and very good looking, and wore
plus-fours, black and white shoes, and one of those grey garments
that later became known as a windcheater. His name was Horton
Smith. His swing was smooth and slow and beautiful, and he putted
with the touch of a violinist. He was two or three down to Fred
Robson when we picked him up but he won in the end by 2 and 1.
I last saw him as he left our hotel after the 1963 match in Atlanta
to return to Detroit. Next morning I read in the paper that he had
died that night. He was one of the classical scholars, so to speak, of
golf.

The first match that I saw as a writer on golf was in 1933 at
Southport and Ainsdale and this, in a sense, is 'where I came in'.
It is common experience to remember more vividly scenes that took
place when the world was new than what happened yesterday. My
recollections of this match, however, have been sharpened by the
fact that some years ago I assembled, from newsreels of the day, a
film entitled 'Great Golfing Occasions', and this match is one of
them. We see again the thousands of people who rushed about the
course, herded, not always successfully, by volunteer stewards
brandishing long bamboo poles with pennants at the end, which
earned them the name of the 'Southport Lancers'. Many had come
to see the golf but many, perhaps more, had come to see the Prince
of Wales, himself a keen golfer, who had come to give the Cup away.
We see him in the end presenting it to dear old J. H. Taylor, non-
playing captain of the British team, almost beside himself with
pride, and we see Hagen with that impudent smile that captured
so many male and female hearts saying, 'We had the Cup on our
table on the *Aquitania* coming over and we had reserved a place for
it on the table going back'. Above all, however, we see what was
perhaps the most desperate finish to any international match played
to this day.

The match as a whole was all square; there was one single to
come in, and this too was all square—with one hole to play. The
protagonists were Densmore Shute (who later went on to win the
Open at St Andrews) and Syd Easterbrook. In the end Shute was
about four and a half feet from the hole in three and Easterbrook a

matter of inches inside him. I do not have to look at the film to remember the scene. It has been imprinted on my mind ever since I watched it. Shute, in the deathly silence that comes from the presence of a vast multitude none of whom is making a sound, missed his putt. So now Easterbrook was left with his four footer, with a nasty left-hand borrow at that, and the complete golfer's nightmare—'This for the entire match'. Even at the age of 24 I remember thinking, 'Better him than me'. Nowadays I doubt whether I could have borne to watch it. Easterbrook holed it like a man, and the Cup was Britain's.

I did not see the following match in America but four years later we were back again at Southport and Ainsdale, with the ground baked hard and a wind of almost gale force blowing. Cotton in practice had done a 64 (his finest hour was to come within a few days when against the full strength of the Americans he won the Open at Carnoustie) and the general note was one of restrained optimism, in which I see that I shared at the time, though for a reason which I reveal with mixed feelings. It was, as I see that I wrote, that the Americans 'have too many wives. Not that they have brought more than one each, but they have brought six in all, together with Master Revolta, aged two. And it is my experience, or rather I have observed it to be other people's, that women on these trips are an encumbrance equivalent roughly to conceding two shots per round.' This forecast, coming, as it did, from a bachelor still in his twenties, proved to be as inaccurate as it was ungallant and the United States won by 7 matches to 3.

Then came the war and it was not until November 1947 that the series was resumed, through the good offices of that perpetual friend of professional golf, Mr. Robert A. Hudson, who sponsored the match at his home club at Portland, Oregon. I did not go over for this but I gather that it rained and rained and rained, and Sam King at the tail end of the procession was the only man to win a point for Britain on either day.

My memories of the 1949 match, which was played at Ganton, near Scarborough, are more of the voyage home from the United States, where I had been watching the Walker Cup match, than of the match itself. The American team came over on the *Queen Elizabeth*, and so did I. Every one of this team had seen some sort of service during the war—a notable record. The smallest of them, Johnny Palmer, had survived thirty bombing missions over Tokyo. For Chick Harbert it was his second crossing in the *Elizabeth*. With 19,000 others he had come over in her during the war. He was still marvelling at the organisation. He and his wife were now occupying a stateroom in which 96 men had slept, 32 at a time in three eight-hour shifts.

In February 1949 Ben Hogan had had his famous motor accident —it is an interesting reflection that had he been wearing a seat belt at the time he would now have been dead some sixteen years— and as a compliment to his almost incredible, though still only partial, recovery, he had been made captain of the American team. His legs were still tightly bandaged and he could walk only with difficulty. We used to spend time in the Turkish bath together and it was here that I began to admire, and perhaps to begin to under-stand, this truly remarkable man. I referred to him once as the non-playing captain, which of course he was, but I could see at once that I had said the wrong thing. His steely blue eyes narrowed and his lips tightened. 'This life is driving me crazy' he said. 'I want to *compete* again'. At that moment the only person who thought he would ever play again, much less compete, was Hogan. What he did later is a matter of golfing history.

I am told that he had some difficulty in persuading his team that the match was not a 'pushover'. If they did think this, they were not unjustified, in view of the 1947 result. Two things combined to cause them to change their minds. The first was that the lowly British led 3—1 in the foursomes on the first day. The second—and it must be remembered that I am giving only personal impressions— was the unduly partisan behaviour of some of the spectators. It is all right to cheer when your own man puts his ball on the green: it is quite inexcusable to let out a roar when the opposition drives into the woods. At any rate on the second day the Americans came out of their corner fighting and a formidable succession of threes began to go up against their names, hole by hole, on the scoreboard. The result was 7—5 in their favour and a match which had frankly proved unsatisfactory from the British point of view from more than one angle was over.

The match at Pinehurst, North Carolina, in 1951 brings back on the other hand the pleasantest of memories. Pinehurst, as its name suggests, is simply a green oasis in a vast desert of pines. It has four golf courses radiating from a central clubhouse; some excellent hotels; a number of homes belonging to citizens whose names are household words in America; a row of shops which includes a stock-broker's office; and that is about all. In Pinehurst golf is everything. The match was played, uniquely, on the Friday and the Sunday. This was because on the Saturday the University of Carolina were

due to play football against Tennessee—a match which I gathered
excited the kind of 'needle' which we in Britain associate with
Celtic *v*. Rangers in Scotland—and nobody, of course, was prepared
to miss it.

Till the Friday we had been sweltering in almost tropical heat,
yet on the morning of the foursomes we woke up to a scene which
might have been December at Gleneagles: an authentic Scotch mist,
limiting visibility to a drive and a brassie; shivering spectators; and
the players blowing on their fingers to keep them warm. It made a
lasting impression on me and perhaps I cannot do better than recall
what I cabled home at the time:

'Among the gallery in the fourth match, bearing no outward and
visible sign connecting him with the proceedings, is a small, dark
man, with grey raincoat, grey cap, grey trousers, and inscrutable
expression, looking somewhat like a Pinkerton detective on unob-
trusive watch for pickpockets. This is the world's greatest golfer,
Ben Hogan, participating in the Ryder Cup match. His partner, the
normally flamboyant Jimmy Demaret, is concealed in a flowing
check Ulster, with a distinctly Sherlock Holmesian air. From time
to time they step forward, undress, give the ball a resounding slam,
and return to anonymity.

'As if this is not enough, the afternoon turns to rain, pouring
relentlessly down on the avenues of silent pines. Sodden spectators,
looking strangely woebegone in their bizarre headgear, trickle back
to the clubhouse; the refreshment tent runs out of "hot dogs"; and
what has so long been a sunny, colourful scene turns to something
approaching a wet Sunday afternoon in Wigan.'

Some of the British team came out very well. Charles Ward and
Arthur Lees played the last six holes of the first round of the foursomes in 3, 3, 2, 5, 3, 3, and eventually won Britain's only point. Lees
went on to win his single—the only man to win two points and one
of very few who have done so in America—while Ward took Hogan
to the 34th. It was only two and a half years after his accident but
I see that I recorded 'The answer to Hogan, in foursomes or singles,
is that, if Hogan means to win—you lose.' I note also that in the
foursomes the Americans played 132 holes between them without a
single six. In the end they won by 9—2, with one match halved, and
a further match, not recorded in the Handbook, was made when the
British captain, Arthur Lacey, married a lady from Pinehurst and
lived happily ever afterwards.

Two years later the Americans came over to Wentworth and here
ensued a tremendous contest. With the foursomes lost by 3—1—and

the one point gained only by a wonderful putt by Fred Daly on the last green—it was clear by lunchtime on Saturday that we were not going to regain the Cup. Then, as so often happens in these team matches, one detected a swing going on simultaneously all over the course. Rapid calculations showed that, if only one or two not unreasonable things might occur, we not only were not going to lose: we might even win. Daly, hero of the match if ever there was one, was round in 66 to polish off Ted Kroll and then, believe it or not, here was Snead, four up with five to play on Weetman, losing all the last five holes and with them the match. This, of course, counted two on a division and there came the sudden realisation that if only Alliss, one down and one to play, could halve and Hunt, one up with one to play, could win, the Cup would change hands.

What ensued made a lasting mark on Alliss, as he has eloquently revealed in his book *Alliss in the Looking Glass*, and one feels that if he had quietly lost his match out in the country the rest of his golfing life might have been different. As it was, in the full ghastly light of publicity, not to be dimmed for many years, he took four from the edge of the green for a six, when even a five would have won the hole and halved the match. Behind him, bringing up the rear, was Hunt and, as the evening shadows fell, he too took three putts and a six, when a five would have won the match. Nevertheless, my own most vivid memory is of an almost comical nature. It concerns that great competitor, Lloyd Mangrum, the American captain, who was in the end beaten by an equally great competitor, at any rate in match play, Eric Brown. The scene was the 7th green, where Mangrum was on the lower level, with a steep bank between him and the hole. He hit it only just to the top and then slowly, slowly it began to gather speed and roll back. He beckoned it on with his finger; it came obediently back to his feet, and without even shifting his stance he putted a second time. A kindly cheer broke out when the second one surmounted the hill but in the end he took four putts—an episode watched by millions on the television and remembered to this day.

The 1955 match took place in the Californian desert, where the light is so bright and the air so clear that what would look bizarre in a more sombre climate looks perfectly natural. Both sexes wear multicoloured clothes and the women wear ridiculous great straw hats and nobody thinks of driving a car of only one colour. I remember the huge practice ground where ball after ball would shower out like white tracers against the blue sky and fall slowly to earth against a background of the 10,000 ft mountains behind. Everything at Thunderbird was larger than life. In the 'buggy stables' they had two hundred electric carts, many with gaily tasselled awnings and a compartment for soft and not-so-soft drinks. When I asked for transport, the man at the door looked round for a moment and said, 'Here. Better take this one'. 'This one' proved to be a beautiful brand new blue and white creation bearing a notice 'You too can have the new 1956 Bel Air Chevrolet'. It had 68 miles on the clock when I took it. I drove it about 500 miles and left it where I found it.

As to the golf, the British team, 'written off' almost unanimously by the critics before they left, did rather well in winning four matches and taking seven of those they lost to the 34th hole or further, but my own recollections are confined to one scene. It is the last green and Fallon and Jacobs are one up on the Americans, Chandler Harper and Jerry Barber. The latter are in some rough grass at the back of the steeply sloping green: the British, in the like, are four or five yards away from the flag on the right. In a moment Fallon would only have to roll the ball across the slope to the hole and the match would be ours. Barber made his chip and the ball, taking ages in its passage, rolled slowly down and down—and into the hole. It was one of the most diabolical shots I have ever seen— and furthermore it was the third time he had done it in 18 holes. If ever a man's face may be said to 'fall', it was Fallon's. He seemed to turn almost grey in a moment. Half a minute later he had holed one of the bravest putts ever made in a Ryder Cup match.

At this time golf in the desert was a comparative novelty. There were, I believe, three courses. Unlimited water, however, had been discovered a few hundred feet down and what had always been called desert was not, in fact, desert at all but extremely fertile soil waiting only for water. In fact, grass grew so quickly that you had only, they declared, to 'spread the seed, apply the water, and jump back'! When we returned four years later to play at the Eldorado club, it was one of many that had risen from the desert in the inter- vening time, and now there are fifteen. Eldorado was a most lavish affair and when I arrived on the preceeding Thursday no fewer than 150 men were still working on the clubhouse, hammering on the roof, creating flower beds and unwrapping the furniture from its covers. The course, however, had been created from a citrus range two years previously and it would have made European golf architects gnash their teeth to learn that only six months and one week later the course was in such perfect condition that it was

possible to take a driver from the fairway. Architects and part
owners of all this were Jimmy Hines, who had been professional at
Thunderbird during the previous match, and Johnny Dawson, a
past Walker Cup player and semi-finalist in the British Amateur
at Sandwich thirty years before. At many of the holes they had put
water hazards round the greens instead of sand traps, on the basis
that you can 'splash' out of sand easily enough with a wedge but
you cannot splash out of water. This led to a curious and unexpected
result. Each year, as the Bermuda grass browned off, they sowed the
course with a finer variety of rye and this year for the first time had
carried out the operation by air. The aviator, nipping off the tops
of two palm trees in the process, had done it all in two days and the
grass was being mown ten days later. The only trouble was that he
also sowed the water hazards and grew a lawn on top of them as
well.

Considering all, the British team did not do as badly as the
figures might indicate. After a heavy buffeting on the *Queen Elizabeth*
and eight days of continuous travel, speech making, and receptions
thereafter, they took a chartered plane from Los Angeles to Palm
Springs, together with a number of supporters and camp followers,
of which I mercifully was not one. Caught at night in a thunder-
storm, the tail end of a hurricane which had been devastating
Mexico, their plane was tossed about among the mountains to such
an extent that their baggage hit the roof and the stewardess was
quickly rendered insensible. They endured nearly an hour of this
before the plane turned back and everyone of them had passed
through that unforgettable moment when they knew that their
end had come. They formed a club called the 'Long Drop Club',
complete with its own tie, and once every year the survivors still
dine together and thank providence that they are alive.

Such were the two matches in the Californian desert. Between
them came the historic match at Lindrick about which I still find
it difficult to write with detachment. It was, beyond all doubt, a
remarkable and well-merited victory for the British team, yet the
taste of victory was not so sweet as it should, and might, have been.
One member of the British team had the ill fortune to let fall an
injudicious observation within hearing of a zealous journalist, who
contrived to turn it overnight into a national 'incident'. The
arrangements made for the American team were grotesquely
inadequate and what they must have thought of us I do not care to
think. When all was over, some of them did not even stay for the
prizegiving and practically none turned up for the dinner.

To conceal these things would be unfair to the reader but it would be equally unfair to deny to the British team the full credit for their performance on the golf course and for the team spirit with which they came back after losing the foursomes by 3—1. When the singles began, a whole succession of 3's at the par-4 first hole appeared on the scoreboard. Yesterday the same thing had happened but the 3's were against the names of the Americans. This time they were against the names of the humble British. Cheer after cheer swept across the course as the putts were holed and one could almost *feel* the uplift pervading the British team, far apart from each other as they might be. At the same time disintegration set in among the Americans and as a team they simply fell apart. Nor do I think this is a harsh verdict: I am sure that all concerned would agree. Only those who were present felt the vague unease. For golfers all over the nation it was a time to rejoice and the victors deserved every pat on the back they received when they got home.

Four years later for the next home match, played at Royal Lytham and St Annes, Dai Rees was again captain and in winning both his singles, against J. Hebert and Ford, played a real captain's innings. The Ryder Cup match had now taken on a different look, which I must confess to have been a great satisfaction to me personally. For years I had been pressing the case for having two 18-hole matches each day instead of one of 36, whether it be in the Ryder Cup, the University match, or any other Cup. It had so often happened that a couple of the four foursomes were virtually over by lunch time and thus fifty per cent of the interest disappeared from the spectators' point of view and a couple of 'processions' wound their weary way round the course in the afternoon. I certainly do not claim any credit for the fact but it remains that the two professional Associations did decide that at Lytham it would be 18-hole matches, with 24 points at stake instead of 12, and, biassed though I may be, I do think that this was universally appreciated—so much so, in fact, that the Walker and Curtis Cups followed suit and the University match too, and now only the final of the Amateur Championship drags its way over 36 holes. We were treated to two wonderful days of man-to-man golf at Lytham. Out of 24 matches only 7 failed to go to the 16th, which is as much as any spectator can ask, and those who had a bad morning lived to make a fresh start in the afternoon. As so often, one shot stands out. In the first series of singles Palmer, British open champion at the time, played Alliss, and here was a real heavyweight contest. Alliss was one up with four to play when Palmer, bunkered beside the green at the 15th, pitched the ball out

—straight into the hole first bounce for a three: a shot almost as diabolical as Barber's at Thunderbird eight years before. They halved the last three holes, and the match, and both were round in 70. Among the spectators was Peter Alliss's father, Percy, a member of the Ryder Cup team in which Rees had played some 27 years before. Old golfers, said a wag, never Dai.

So finally we come to Atlanta two years ago and the East Lake course, home of the great Bobby Jones—Bob to the Americans but never to us—and here the form of the contest has taken on another change. All these international contests had been played, as seemed natural when they started, by foursomes and singles. Foursomes, however, are a game so strange in America that a vast percentage of club golfers have never heard of them, while those who have call them 'Scotch foursomes'. I must have been to the United States at least twenty times but it is a fact that I have never seen anyone play a foursome other than in international contests. The British were loth to give them up: on the other hand only those Americans who had previously played in the Ryder Cup had ever played one. In day-to-day golf nobody in America plays anything but fourballs. Logically, therefore, and to the benefit of the gate, the match was now extended to three days, with two singles, two foursomes and two fourballs, all over 18 holes, and now 32 points were at stake instead of the original 12.

Scoring in fourballs is bound to be low in this sort of company but it did seem a little hard when O'Connor and Coles, playing Palmer and Finsterwald, went out in 34, which is not all that bad, and found themselves five down! The hero of these three days, however, was Alliss. On his half with Palmer at Lytham he recorded later in his book, accurately and without lack of modesty, 'I didn't halve with Palmer. Palmer halved with me'. Now here he was, playing Palmer again in his own country, and the American captain at that. It was a wonderful match and Alliss's putt on the 17th, following a longer one by Palmer, was beyond praise. He held him off and beat him by one hole. Not many people have a record like that against Palmer!

2 Golf Promotion—1965 Style

By
GEOFFREY COUSINS

AMONG THE many thousands who swarmed over the Birkdale sand-hills during three exciting October days there were no doubt a few able to contrast the Ryder Cup scenes of 1965 with those of the early days of Anglo-American golf battles. There was not, strange though it may seem, a tremendous difference in quantity—the really big golf occasion thirty or forty years ago could always be certain of attracting large crowds, and there was one great day at Southport and Ainsdale course when 18,000 people paid to see the Ryder Cup singles and uncounted thousands more gate-crashed on to the links to see, not the golfers, but the Prince of Wales. But there was a big difference in the attitude of the spectators to the golf and the attitude of the promoters to the spectators. The golf-watchers of the 1920's were mainly people who played the game and understood it well, or at least were well acquainted with it by family influences. And except on very big occasions, and sometimes not even then, the followers were left to look after themselves, amenities and facilities outside the clubhouse being usually inadequate or non-existent.

Nowadays the spectator can be either a keen golfer, a keen television fan, or just one who loves a spectacle no matter what the subject. And he demands and gets not only value for money in what he witnesses, but also, within limits, an adequate degree of comfort and service from the promoters. Forty years ago golf-watching was an esoteric pastime and no promoter, least of all those concerned with amateur events, worried very much about the spectator. If the occasion were important enough, a local caterer might be commissioned to provide food and drink in a tent. There were very few cars of course, and there was usually a field to be hired from a farmer-member of the club. If there were any attempt at all to provide toilet facilities it was usually limited to a few yards of flapping hessian draped on poles in some obscure woody corner. Crowd control was almost non-existent, and if a really large gallery assembled to watch a particularly good match some club members would be recruited to walk around with red flags, which at least had the advantage of giving them front-row positions to watch the putting. Had any member of an organising committee (supposing one had existed)

B

suggested the provision of any further facilities for the spectator he would have been laughed to scorn. The fact was that those who came to watch rarely paid anything. Those who had the entrée to the clubhouse were all right, Jack. The rest could fend for themselves.

It is almost incredible that the Championship Committee of the Royal and Ancient Golf Club of St. Andrews did not charge gate-money for the Amateur and Open Championships until 1926. And the figures make interesting reading today. For the whole week of the Amateur at Muirfield, in the middle of the great golfing stretch of coast near Edinburgh, 9,000 people paid £996. At Lytham and St. Annes, in the Open won by Bobby Jones, 12,000 paid £1,365 in three days. It is estimated that at least 60,000 watched the Ryder Cup match and Practice of 1965. It is interesting to note that Peter Thomson's first prize in the Open Championship of 1965, was £400 more than that total Lytham gate of 1926.

As public interest increased and crowds grew larger it became incumbent on organisers to cater for the great majority who could not gain admittance to the 'host' club premises, and therefore con- stituted a multitude to be supplied with loaves and fishes by outside caterers. There was also ever-increasing pressure on promoters to provide adequate and decent toilet facilities, car-parking, etc. And crowd control passed out of the 'red flag' era to become a matter for ropes, fences and small armies of stewards. For many years, it must be said, the enthusiasm of the promoters lagged behind the needs of the public. The most enterprising sponsors did their best to ensure comfort for the spectators, and catering for golf became big business for a few enterprising firms. But the real breakthrough did not come until 1962, and then in a dramatic way with the promotion of the first Senior Service tournament at Dalmahoy, near Edinburgh. In a spacious area adjoining the clubhouse the promoters arranged a complete symmetrical and attractive-looking golf village of white clean canvas, which provided every possible facility, including a ladies' 'powder room' of ample proportions, discreet appearance and luxurious appointments. There were excellent bars and luncheon marquees, a television tent, rest pavilions, fashion shows, hot and cold running water, flush toilets—the lot. At various points on the course large tubular-steel stands were erected and the information service from the course achieved a record for completeness and clarity. And the Senior Service Festival of Golf saw the introduction of periscopes to this country.

I think it true to say that the Senior Service 'golf village' at

Dalmahoy provided a blue print for tournament planners. But since the best ideas in the world are capable of improvement the organisers of the Ryder Cup match of 1965 set a new standard in their successful efforts to provide what has generally been hailed as a fantastically efficient setting at Birkdale. It must have been some satisfaction to Mr. R. Binnie Clark, the architect of the Dalmahoy 'village', that he was also concerned in the Ryder Cup 'set-up'. For Senior Service contributed a number of new ideas to the Birkdale promotion, including scoring cars driven by leading lady golfers to keep the public in constant touch with each match, an animated location board showing at a glance where all matches were on the course and now the players stood, and an observation tower for Press and photographers commanding extensive views of the course.

These contributions by Mr. Clark and the Gallaher organisation were welcomed by the Ryder Cup sponsor, Mr. Brian Park, a former Captain of Royal Birkdale, because he realised that if the 1965 Ryder Cup week was to be the success he hoped for, it must depend on the efforts of many people, all with one aim in view. Planning for the Ryder Cup began in the mind of Mr. Park more than two years beforehand when in the autumn of 1963 his offer to guarantee the 1965 contest was accepted by the Professional Golfers' Association. From the start he was determined that the promotion should set new standards not only for Britain but also for the world, in golf organisation and presentation.

He travelled to the United States to see the best that country had to offer—and returned with a confidence, not subsequently misplaced, that we could do all that the American's could do—and more. But he was impressed by one thing—the size of the souvenir programmes which for years had been an integral part of big golf promotion in the States. And when he formed his Ryder Cup Committee and began putting various ideas into shape, one of his first moves was to entrust the production of a mammoth programme to George Simms, a director of Exclusive Press Features Ltd., the firm which had done a great deal in connection with the Senior Service promotions and other big tournaments, and had been engaged as promotional and publicity advisers to the Ryder Cup Committee.

There were two imponderables about this programme job. Would potential advertisers support it to a profitable extent? Would the public buy these 5s. 'magazines' in sufficient numbers? The answer to both questions was 'Yes', and George Simms and his assistant editor, Christopher Berry, set their own particular Ryder Cup standard. With contributions on various aspects of the match by golf writers on both sides of the Atlantic, a large pull-out coloured plan of the Birkdale links, pen-pictures and photographs of the players and the full records of past Ryder Cup matches, this 160-page venture was far and away the largest and most ambitious undertaking of the kind ever attempted in British golf. If the magnificence of the programme astonished the many thousands of spectators, they were astounded by the extent of the services which had been assembled, mainly under canvas, on the stretch of ground between the clubhouse and the Liverpool–Southport road. There were, of course, the old favourites—the resplendent flower-bordered caravans of the leading banks in a rank facing the clubhouse. And the luncheon marquees, the information tent, the lost-property tent, the ubiquitous and essential lavatories, the first-aid tent, the Golf Trade exhibition, and the travelling Post Office. But a new note was struck by the installation of tastefully designed pavilions hired by clubs, associations and even business firms for the entertainment of members and clients. More than a dozen of these pavilions, which are often in use at race meetings and agricultural shows, made a splash of opulent colour and no doubt repaid handsomely for the modest hiring fees. These and other well-sited tents and caravans helped to constitute an encampment far exceeding in size and comprehensiveness anything hitherto seen at a golf course. But it was not all show. In the background were all kinds of modern aids to efficiency working for the smooth running of the event. The biggest Press pavilion ever seen on this side of the Atlantic, a massive wooden structure, was occupied by the largest number of golf writers ever to attend a big event in Britain. They had the benefit of the smartest and most thorough service from the course in the shape of information of all kinds. Not only was the score of each hole of every match available in the Press room immediately the players walked off a green, but there was also available the record of what clubs the players had used for the various shots.

There were many other elaborations on the same theme—service to the public. Looking back on this match, recalling the milling thousands who lined the sandhills and ringed the greens of the Birkdale links, picturing again the colour and massiveness of the encampment, I can say without fear of contradiction that never before, in the history of big golf promotion anywhere in the world, was so much done for so many as in the Ryder Cup matches of 1965 at Royal Birkdale.

3   BIRKDALE
—Queen in a Golfing Paradise

A SAGA OF THE SANDHILLS

THE ENTHUSIASM with which Birkdale members and officers supported the Ryder Cup operation, and their efforts in the past in connection with two Open Championships and many important amateur events, including a Walker Cup match, were typical of a club which has always been progressive in outlook and practical in the approach to all kinds of problems and situations. When we consider how much work goes into the organisation of even one big event every three or four years, which is the usual task confronting the committee of a 'championship' golf club, we might well feel astonished that Birkdale could put on the Open Championship and the Ryder Cup in the space of four months and still look forward with undiminished vigour to the Carling World Championship due there in the following year. It is true, of course, that the nucleus of the organisation is always there, ready to be built on for each successive promotion. And it cannot be denied that Birkdale has natural advantages of situation and environment which are denied some other championship clubs. Nevertheless, no one who has ever been to a big show there can ever have been in doubt that everyone concerned is always on the ball and geared for action.

Everyone who went to the Ryder Cup match and saw Birkdale for the first time must have realised how fortunate the club was to possess such natural golf country and have its headquarters so well situated and so accessible for transport. The country itself, of course, is marvellous. A time-honoured phrase uttered more than a century ago in reference to a proposed golf course in the South of England— 'Providence obviously destined this for a golf course'—could be applied with even greater force to that sandy paradise which stretches for miles along the coast between Liverpool and Southport. The sand, silted up by the estuaries of the Mersey and the Ribble, lies firm, hard and wide on the seashore, ideal for motor racing and car picnics; but further inland piles up into ranges of sandhills which stretch as far as the eye can see. This mass of dunes, bound together by marram and other tenuous grasses and masses of willow scrub and vegetation, accommodates half a dozen golf courses and there is room for as many more, but none is more conveniently situated or more efficiently designed than the Royal Birkdale links.

Birkdale indeed has come a long way since 1889, when nine Southport business men founded the club and began operations with a modest nine-hole course and a one-room 'clubhouse' rented at 4s. a week. The big days of Birkdale began soon after the Great War, when the cotton boom was at its height and Southport vied with Lytham as a dormitory for Manchester business men. Fine houses were built along and near the Southport–Liverpool road, and with the onset of affluence the members of Birkdale began to extend their ideas of what was fitting in both course and clubhouse. In 1931 two projects were started—the erection of an entirely new clubhouse and the complete redesigning of the course. John Henry Taylor, five times open champion and his fellow-Devonian Fred Hawtree, who were partners in a firm of golf course architects, were called in and produced the present-day layout. It is important to remember, in view of the utter fitness of Birkdale for accommodating and handling large crowds, that the vital feature of the new design was that the valleys between ridges of sandhills were used as fairways. Until then some of the holes had traversed sandhills, giving a number of blind shots and a lot of laborious climbing. The new design not only made maximum use of the valleys but was also arranged in two nine-hole loops, both starting and finishing at the clubhouse. This arrangement, sparing the legs of the members, made their golf more pleasant and less frustrating, and facilitated the movement and control of large crowds at big events. At the same time a clubhouse of considerable size, designed for the job, took shape in a commanding position, to announce to everyone that Birkdale was ready in every way to be considered as a championship club. That career began modestly enough with the English Ladies' Championship in 1935, followed by the Boys' Championship in 1936, and proceeding in stages of importance to the point where the course was selected for the Open Championship of 1940. The war held up that honour for 14 years but in the meantime the Amateur Championship of 1946 was played at Birkdale and in 1951—the year that the appellation 'Royal' was conferred on the club—a great and exciting Walker Cup match was played there.

With all these successes it might be thought that the Birkdale members would be satisfied that their course and clubhouse were equal to all requirements. But golf never stands still and the demands of the game and its devotees become ever greater. The 1961 Open Championship at Birkdale was badly affected by the weather, but while this could not be foreseen it did emphasise certain deficiencies which the officers and members, with typical business sense, decided to put right. It was conceded that if the club wished to maintain its reputation for putting on big golf in a satisfactory way, it must keep pace with the ever-rising standards of promotion. In no other was way it possible to satisfy the crowds clamouring for sustenance, elbow-room and information. With typical Birkdale keenness, a start was made with the clubhouse, with big extensions and internal alterations. Then a major reconstruction of the course —with F. W. Hawtree, son of J. H. Taylor's partner, as the architect. And at the same time a thorough reorganisation of the environs of the club to accommodate more and more spectators, more and more cars, more and more services, in better and better comfort. The outcome, tested at the Open Championship so magnificently won by Peter Thomson, was seen in full fruition in this great Ryder Cup match, and left no doubt that the officials and members of Royal Birkdale, imbued with the same spirit which had actuated their founders 76 years before, had 'done it again'.

No one can deny that the Birkdale links as redesigned provide one of the greatest tests of golf in Britain. The principal item of reconstruction was an entirely new short hole in virgin country towards the sea. Room for the inclusion of this hole—numbered 12 —was made by obliterating the short 17th. And this in turn enabled Mr. Hawtree to lengthen and re-design the 18th to convert it into a challenging dogleg of 513 yards. The 14th hole, renumbered 15, was also lengthened, and so Royal Birkdale now had a finishing stretch of six holes, four of more than 500 yards. In this way Birkdale has kept pace with the increasing power and skill of the golfer. But at the same time the designer improved the lot of the spectator. Six teeing-grounds were re-sited to allow onlookers to move freely from hole to hole. The former painful and laborious dashing through willow scrub was eliminated by bulldozing wide paths through the sandhills, and the institution of a regular traffic system made it possible for more spectators to see more shots. It also eased considerably the efforts of the stewards, and facilitated the progress of matches. At various points on the course natural stands were provided by making turfed banks behind greens, and there were also tubular-steel grandstands at places of maximum interest—for instance at either side of the home green. So Birkdale was perfectly equipped for the big occasion. The players were tested to the utmost and their efforts could be watched in comfort by fans well fed, well parked and well served—better treated, indeed, than any collection of spectators had ever been in the past.

Birkdale has always been a daunting course for all but the best golfers, and even the best golfers must treat it with respect. Birkdale, that is, from the back tees as used in the Ryder Cup match and, earlier that year, in the Open Championship. Every club, for the sake of its members, forgets about the back tees for all but a few weeks of the year, and there are medal, middle and forward tees at Birkdale to suit all grades of player. Yet, from whatever tee is chosen, the hazards are there, to be circumvented or endured. For the championship contender using the very back tees the problem is to make the drive both big and accurate. Big, because many of the carries demand maximum power. Accurate, because placing of the drive is of paramount importance, as it should be on every well-designed links. But even when the ball has finished in the selected place the second shot to the green, although made possible, is never made easy.

All the members of the British team were familiar with the new Birkdale, but to most of the Americans it was new country in every sense of the phrase. The wonder with which they first surveyed the mass of sandhills stretching to the horizon, and tried to visualise fairways and greens mostly hidden from view, was exceeded only by the admiration expressed after close acquaintance with the layout.

Although Mr. Hawtree had done wonders in reconciling the needs of spectators and organisers with the requirements of good planning, it was necessary for the high back teeing-ground used in the Open Championship of 1961, and for other events prior to the reconstruction, to be abandoned in favour of the original first tee, hard by the road leading to the clubhouse. The high back tee narrowed the bottle-neck between 'Jutland', the sandhill breaking the fairway on the left, and the out-of-bounds fence on the right, and made it extremely difficult to get the ball into the right position for the second shot to a green half hidden by another big sandhill. Nevertheless the hole from the shorter right-hand tee, although slightly easing the problem of the drive, was still a good test, and naturally the Americans spent a lot of time on it in practice. They must also have been impressed by the way in which the soaring sandhills had been utilised for the high tees featured at the majority of the holes. These high trees are intimidating and at the same time exhilarating. Let us stand for example, imaginative driver in hand, on the eighth tee, and survey what lies before us. There is a nasty bunker on the left, a whole row of equally menacing hazards on the right, and beyond them on either side stretches the willow scrub and the knee-deep tufted grass on the slopes of the sandhills. The fairway swerves to the left, and there in the distance, cocked up on its plateau in a ring of bunkers is the green, 459 yards away. The ordinary mortal will be well satisfied to get home in two, and if the willow scrub or the sand claims him he can say goodbye to par.

This is typical of the golf which Birkdale offers. The ninth is untypical, since it provides the only 'blind' drive on the course, but it is none the less a good Birkdale hole, with a deceptively wide fairway. There is actually very little scope for the drive. One too far left will finish in bad rough and a ball too far right will be gathered by steeply sloping ground and run into trouble. At all other holes the challenge is visible, and some of them are formidable. Take for instance the tenth, which has been made more difficult by a shift of tee, again necessitated by organisation for the big occasion. In this case the tee has been moved from the platform near the ninth green to a similar eminence towards the sea. This turns a modest bend into an acute dogleg, almost a right angle, and brings even more prominently into play the menacing sandhill on the left with its cunningly placed bunker. Indeed, what the designer lost at the first hole he gained at the tenth, where the golfer who gets his drive just right and makes his four should be very well satisfied.

Probably the hole which most pleased the Americans was the new short 12th, constructed from virgin sandhills to replace the eliminated short 17th. This new hole of 190 yards has plenty of room for error but invites a teeshot pitched well up to the green. It might be a different hole in mid-summer drought conditions because the ground slopes steeply down from the bank at the back of the green. But this was October after a wet summer.

Another change of tee-position made to facilitate movement of galleries has improved the 13th, 60 yards longer and bending gradually to the right. The 15th, at 536 yards the longest hole of the new Birkdale, illustrates the cunning of good design. More than a dozen bunkers are placed in just the right (or, from another point of view, the wrong) positions, and those causing most trouble are on the left of the fairway where the drives finish. They squeeze the player between sand and the right-hand jungle rough, and make the big hitter think twice before he has a go for a birdie.

We are now in the middle of Birkdale's intimidating finish. The 13th and 15th holes are both over 500 yards. The 16th represents a temporary relief in the matter of length but not in difficulty, for there is tremendous carry with the additional task of steering past deep ferocious willow scrub and sand on the right. During one round of the Open Championship of 1961, Arnold Palmer failed to do this but he made the green with a terrific recovery shot from an apparently impossible situation, and those who pass by are reminded of this feat by a commemoration plate.

The 17th comes back to the 500-yard standard, and that brings us to the home hole, increased to 513 yards and converted into a decided dogleg by moving the tee well to the right of its old position. This was facilitated by the disappearance of the short 17th, and the result is as great a finishing hole as one could imagine.

This, then, was the setting for the Great Ryder Cup match of 1965. The famous links in its framework of sandhills, the great encampment of marquees, tents, pavilions, caravans and cabins, the gleaming ranks of cars twinkling in the sunshine, the masses of people streaming after the various matches. Add to this the air of excitement inseparable from a big occasion, and you have the golf picture of the year.

4 Samuel Ryder Sowed the Seed

IT IS possible to take a cynical view of Samuel Ryder and regard him as merely a commercially minded seed merchant who got a tremendous amount of publicity for the price of a gold cup. And it is true that Samuel Ryder did less, in terms of money, for British professional golf than some modern sponsors of these matches. Their gestures had to be generous, to the tune of five figures, to overcome some of the financial problems inherited by the Professional Golfers' Association when they accepted Ryder's golf cup without endowment. For years the task of meeting the cost of sending teams to the States, and entertaining American teams here, was a biennial headache, a constant drive to make ends meet. Nowadays the Ryder Cup means big money and the headaches are over, which enables us to take an honest view of Samuel Ryder and admire him as a genius who was years ahead of his time and gave British golf a much-needed shot in the arm to stimulate the right kind of growth. Which is what one might expect from a successful business man who, for all his commercial shrewdness and strong will, combined both humour and humanity in his tall, spare frame.

We have no doubt that if Samuel Ryder had been asked to endow his trophy he would have done so. But he was too good a business man not to appreciate a bargain. It was his instinct for a bargain and his ingrained business ability which led him to make a fortune from penny packets of seeds. He spent his early working life in the family corn-chandler's business at Manchester and came up one day with a startling suggestion. Instead of selling flower and vegetable seeds by weight, why not put small quantities into penny packets? It would be a bargain no one could resist, he argued. Samuel was right, of course. But he had to leave the family firm and set up his own business at St. Albans to prove it. Success came quickly and with it the trappings of success, including membership of the local golf club, in this case Verulam. Samuel Ryder was no player, but if his own golf was inconspicuous he was a great admirer of proficiency in others, and in the years immediately following the Great War he took a keen interest in Abe Mitchell, destined to go down in history as the greatest golfer who never won the Open. But in the 1920's Ryder thought, as we all did at the time, that Mitchell must win the Open, and the shrewd seed-merchant realised what we all know today, that a professional who had to look after a shop, make clubs and teach duffers could not give proper attention to playing golf of championship standard.

It may be imagined that Samuel Ryder's decision to appoint Mitchell as his private coach seemed at the time to be quixotic action, but the appointment was made purely to allow Abe to concentrate on playing, and one thing led to another until one day in 1926 there was talk among the professionals of a match against the United States on the lines of the Walker Cup series for amateurs. Ryder promised to provide a trophy, the first match was fixed to be played in America in 1927, Abe Mitchell was appointed British captain and—one of life's ironies—was taken ill on the boat train to Southampton and had to be left behind.

Mitchell never won the Open, either. But if Samuel Ryder failed to achieve his original object in becoming a golf patron, he lived to see Britain win his trophy twice. He sowed a seed which blossomed at Moortown in 1929, at Southport in 1933 and years later at Lindrick in 1957. And his faith in the ability of British golfers to beat the Americans, if they were given an equal chance, never wavered. The divorce of the tournament player from the chores of a golf club job, which he achieved by his offer to Abe Mitchell, is now common practice.

When Samuel Ryder died in 1936 at the age of 77 he was remembered with affection by the PGA and its members. And the slender golf trophy remains today a monument to the man who realised that something had to be done for British golf and had the enterprise to do it.

5 Warming Up

If the Ryder Cup match takes place on Thursday, Friday and Saturday why start the ball rolling on Monday? The answer, apart from the natural desire of the promoters to explore every possible means of increasing the total 'gate', lies in the peculiar habits of the enthusiastic spectator. Making a week of it, indeed, is very popular with those people who take their golf-watching seriously. A great number earmark part of their annual holidays for the occasion. There are also those fortunate people who can take a week off at any time, and the still more fortunate individuals who find business interests and the Ryder Cup match coinciding. Some hardened veterans at the game will argue, with some truth, that one can see more of the players during the three days of practice than on the three match-days. Nevertheless, the thrill of the actual encounter is the real reason for the expedition, and he who comes on Mondays and stays till Saturday has the best of both worlds.

So it was that on Monday the 4th of October there were plenty of people on the Royal Birkdale links having what was for many of them the first sight of an American golf team in action; and for practically everybody a first sight of the majority of the visiting players. The Americans had flown in the previous day from the United States, via London Airport, and joined their British rivals in a convivial Sunday get-together which did everyone a power of good but made no one forget the main purpose of the exercise. And on the Monday morning, with the fraternising over, it was down to business.

The Americans were two short for this first practice session. Tony Lema, having represented America, with Jack Nicklaus, in the Canada Cup at Madrid, had been delayed on his flight from Spain and did not arrive until that evening. And, more serious, Johnny Pott, one of the newcomers to the U.S. team, was in the hands of a masseur. Playing on a New York course just before leaving for Britain, Johnny had hurt his side and put it down to a wrenched muscle which would soon respond to treatment. The trouble, as it transpired, was more serious. Johnny had heat treatment and massage twice on Sunday and twice on Monday before and after a few shots with a No. 8 iron which convinced him he was not yet in shape for hitting a golf ball in anger. So Byron Nelson, the American captain, wisely decided he should have more treatment and delay serious work until all risk of aggravating the injury had disappeared.

Nelson, whom we now introduce, was returning to familiar country, for it was on the neighbouring Southport and Ainsdale links in 1937 that he played in the Ryder Cup match and, incidentally, lost in the singles to a Welshman named Dai Rees, a youngster still in his 'teens who was then British match-play champion. We had a chat with Byron about those far-off days and he alluded to the tremendous difference between then and now in golf promotion and public interest in the game. He was greatly impressed by the whole arrangements for this match, alluded to the British use of canvas in large quantities, and paid British promotion a compliment by hinting that there were plenty of new ideas which could be incorporated in the organisation for the 1967 Ryder Cup matches, to be played at Houston in his native Texas. We also got the impression that the British caddie would be a useful export to the United States. Saying that his men had been helped tremendously by their caddies in getting to know the course, Nelson added: 'We always like your caddies. They know the game.' All the caddies, by the way, were looking very smart indeed in their maroon-coloured track suits. For years the British caddie has been a familiar but nondescript figure, the very antithesis of uniformity. In America, on the other hand, the uniform is in widespread use, and hides the identity of all kinds of youths, from college students to newsboys, who cannot fail to gain valuable experience in the game by performing these part-time or full-time duties. A thought for British promoters and clubs.

Talking with the two captains after this first practice day we received an impression of two widely different characters. Nelson, chubby of face, portly of build, had the urbanity of an impresario and the shrewd discretion of a financier. Weetman, hard of jaw and muscle (as one would expect a fully trained golfer eight years the younger), had the frankness and forthrightness we had come to expect from 'The Shropshire Lad'. Byron would not be drawn on how his men had scored, contenting himself with generalities. 'Palmer and Boros were both level par when I left them at the sixth.' 'No one, I believe, had a bogey' (which, in America, is one over par). And so on. But he went into meticulous detail about the five holes he played with Boros, Palmer and Dave Marr, borrowing one of their clubs for each shot. His description of his play at the third hole, where he picked up after an 'air shot' at a ball suspended in Birkdale's knee-deep willow scrub, was certainly amusing, but probably designed to keep us from inquiring too closely into the performances of his players.

Weetman, on the other hand, dropped his guard and threw his punches, as we might imagine he did during his brief career as an amateur boxer, before he took to golf for his own profit and our rich entertainment. He rattled off all the scores and was at pains to emphasise that O'Connor's 68 included a seven at the 13th. O'Connor and Alliss had a better-ball score of 64 against 68 by Thomas and Will. Another good individual score was 68 by Neil Coles who, with Bernard Hunt, was round in a better-ball score of 66 to beat Lionel Platts (69) and Peter Butler. Jimmy Martin, said Weetman, took 72, but he also described Martin as a great player in a wind and expressed the hope that the wind would start blowing. Pressed to define his attitude to a wind he came out boldly with 'the harder it blows the better I'll be pleased.' 'You'd like a gale?' we asked. 'Yes, a gale,' was the uncompromising reply.

On another subject he was equally emphatic. 'The condition of Birkdale is fantastic for a seaside course,' he complained. 'I've never seen it play so long. Too many fertilisers have made it into practically parkland underfoot. There were six holes, certainly four, where it was impossible to get up in two shots today.' We got the idea that Weetman would have liked the greenkeeper to mow the fairways close and shave the greens. But the state of the course is always in the hands of the host club, just as a Test match pitch depends on the technique of the local groundsman. Birkdale's lush condition, after all, was as much the result of a wet summer as over-enthusiasm by the greens committee. Nevertheless, with memories of Ganton in 1959, when the club dammed a stream, used water guns to soak the fairways, and generally handed the Cup to the Americans on a plate, we could not help feeling, with Weetman, that Nature and the greenkeeper both had made Nelson and his battle squadron feel at home.

Weetman's reference to holes out of range was open to question. Nelson declared that his men could get up at every hole. But having seen the mighty Boros chip twice for his third shot we were equally doubtful of this Byronic belittling of Birkdale. The truth, as is usual between conflicting statements, lay somewhere between the two. It is time to leave the Captains and concentrate on the performances of their men, but not before quoting these declarations of faith:

Weetman: My fellows all know Birkdale inside out. Each plays the game in his own way and can quite well be left to do it without any interference from me. I have more or less made up my mind about foursome partnerships, and there'll be as little swopping and changing as can be during the actual matches. I shall walk round the course keeping an eye on everything, and I'm sure every man in the team is out to win—to do his best.

Nelson (who had previously discussed Johnny Pott's injury and Ken Venturi's operation-scarred hands): I have only one worry. Or perhaps I should say one problem. This is the first time I have acted as Captain of a Ryder Cup team and I want to do a good job. I want to arrange everything—pairings, partnerships and matches—to the best advantage of our side. And once the matches start my concern will be to get all the boys playing at their best, so far as one human being can do it.

So we came to the second day—another lovely day of this Indian summer which everyone was hoping would stay at least until the week-end. All day long the sun shone, all day long the course and the clubhouse and its environs seethed with activity. All day long the enthusiasts poured into Southport. These fall into three well-defined categories. There are the good-time play-boy types who for the first three days at any rate will watch the players for an hour or two but for most of the time will be performing themselves on one or other of the neighbouring courses. Then there are the earnest, dedicated spectators who spend the whole of every day at head-quarters. If there are players to watch, they'll watch them. And in between times they wander around, looking at the tented village, sampling goods in the Trade exhibition, cashing cheques at one or other of the half-dozen bank mobile branches, or gazing at the scoreboard still innocent of figures. And the third category embraces the photographers and cine fans. Festooned with cameras, light-meters, lens cases and filter holders, they spend hours on the practice ground and on the course snapping and whirring away to their hearts' content. Making hay, in fact, while the sun shines, because snapping and whirring are severely frowned upon during the matches.

The hang-around type spent a lot of time on this second day examining the gimmicks and the trimmings, and the dress rehearsal of the Senior Service 'Mini-Mokes' came in for much attention, mainly, we assume, because they were being driven by eight attractive lady golfers. They were to be used as scoring cars, each carrying an operating crew of four, including a scorer, an observer, and a radio operator using a frequency differing from the main *Daily Express* walkie-talkie communications. Each car carried a large scoreboard on which was recorded not only the hole-to-hole score and position of the game it was following, but also the overall position of the match. With the *Daily Express* walkie-talkie system feeding the main scoreboard, and the giant Senior Service animated location board showing the plan of the course, the whereabouts of each game and the state of the game, no one could say that anything had been left wanting in the task of keeping everyone informed. Even those who rested awhile in the various tents and marquees had close-circuit television to keep them in touch with the progress of events.

The two captains were again in confident mood when the second day's practice ended, although it was difficult to imagine Byron Nelson being quite happy over the condition of Johnny Pott. Johnny came out to hit a few shots but he was obviously in trouble. He told his captain he just could not play yet awhile and Nelson ordered more rest and hospital treatment.

Byron was again cagey on the question of his players' scores, but Weetman again had no inhibitions. He was pleased with a return to form of Butler and Platts, who had a better-ball score of 65, Platts doing the first nine holes in 32. O'Connor and Alliss were also round in 65, and Coles and Hunt were playing very well. Another cause for satisfaction for Weetman was his successful bid to have the fairways cut. They were trimmed and that, thought Weetman, would eliminate the element of luck in the long game. Weetman's general feeling was that, with the two sides well matched in the driving, the contest might well depend on the pitching and putting.

So we came to the dawn of the third day and it was a case of all systems go in a rehearsal for the great contest. Last-minute surveys of all the things which might go wrong, urgent calls of various key men in the operation. Will Mr. Brian Park please report to reception. Telephone call for Mr. Binnie Clark of Gallaher's. Will someone ring up the printers and say what about those extra programmes. One of the hirers of the much-admired prestige pavilions was hotfoot in search of the sign-writer to label his particular headquarters. George Simms, the Press Officer, was commuting at great speed between his caravan office, the Press room and the clubhouse, calling the two captains to separate Press conferences and dealing with last-minute applications for Press facilities. Probably the only calm, unworried individuals connected with the match were the players. They were out on the course engaged in foursomes—or, as the Americans would say, Scotch foursomes. In the United States the fourball match is a foursome, for in that country the two-ball game is never played except on these international occasions.

C

All ten British players were engaged but only eight Americans, for there was no partner for Tommy Jacobs. Johnny Pott was still in the hands of masseurs and doctors and while his team-mates were still on the course came the sad news—Johnny was a non-starter. What everyone had feared—because no one in the British team wanted the Americans to be incapacitated in any way—had happened. There were various reports. Pott would not play. Mike Souchak, the first alternate, would fly over as substitute. All was conjecture until Byron Nelson, looking graver than is his wont, appeared in the Press room, shepherded by the indefatigable George Simms, to give the 'gen'.

The United States captain, with clinical exactitude, said that an X-ray examination had shown that Johnny had ruptured an intercostal muscle. This, he said, was one of two muscles on either side of a rib. One had been ruptured—which one was in doubt—but there was no doubt about the verdict. Pott had been forbidden to play golf for at least ten days, and that was that. 'He's horribly upset,' said Nelson, 'and so are we. Naturally I had a talk about the problem with Harry Weetman and your PGA, and was given freedom, as indeed it was allowed by the rules of the match, to call on Mike Souchak to fill the gap. But after I had had a little meeting with my players on the course I decided that we would stay as we are— nine players instead of ten.' The U.S. Captain's reasons were logical. Mike Souchak, even if he could be contacted and were free of tournament commitments—and he was believed to be in Porto Rico—could not possibly get to Southport before Friday. He would be fatigued by the travelling, would have next to no opportunity to get knowledge of the course or accustom himself to climatic conditions, and even then could only be considered for the singles. 'We know from experience how necessary it is to have a little time to settle down and look around,' explained Nelson, 'and the arguments against sending for Souchak are unanswerable. We have nine good, fit men (Ken Venturi is playing magnificently, better than I had hoped) and we'll play the match with those nine.'

Brave words. But Captain Nelson did not disguise the fact that the absence of Pott would throw an additional weight on the rest of the team. His men, he explained, were not used to playing more than one round a day, and his scope for ringing the changes to give some a rest had been exactly halved.

With Pott on the sidelines Nelson's problems about his foursome order of play were practically solved, for Tommy Jacobs was not in such good form as the rest, and, as it proved, he was the odd man out for the first day. Weetman, on the other hand, was having difficulty in making up his mind. After the morning practice he still confessed himself in a quandry. He had sent out what we all regarded as his 'certs' in a sixsome—Alliss and O'Connor, Hunt and Coles, Thomas and Will. And the other match, which he watched with some care, saw Hitchcock and Martin playing against Butler and Platts. 'They're all playing so well that it's tough to have to leave out two,' mourned Weetman at the end of the round. But it had to be done, and after great consideration Weetman decided it must be Hitchcock and Martin. There were still five more chances for these two, but Thursday morning's order was settled. It was time for the two hundred golf writers and news men who had descended on Birkdale to have an opportunity, which might not occur again, to talk collectively with the members of the two teams. A pleasant series of chats in a relaxed atmosphere, and everyone dispersed, with the sun still shining in the clear autumn sky, to ponder upon the prospects and pray with equal voice for a continuance of this Indian summer.

6 A Wonderful, Incredible, Day

The prayers were answered, and thirteen thousand spectators went home tired but happy after the foursomes. They had had a great day of golf-watching in perfect weather, had seen magnificent, even incredible, scoring, and were satisfied that Britain, having halved the day's honours, were still in the match with more than a chance.

It was indeed a wonderful day. The mist and heavy dew which had provided difficult conditions for the Wednesday practice rounds were things of the past. A very light breeze whispered balmily from the South, and although the sky was overcast at the start, the sun soon broke through to shine splendidly, benevolently and impartially throughout the day. The flags at the club masthead and on the various pavilions contributed to the gaiety of the occasion and the intricate colour scheme. So did the striped awnings and the opulent glitter of the bank caravans. So did the blue pullovers of the British players and the yellow of the Americans. There were the usual scenes at the start and even at that early hour, 8.30 a.m., many hundreds of spectators had assembled to watch the opening drives. On the first teeing-ground, with a massive policeman guarding the sacred patch of grass, was assembled a party of notables—the two captains, officials of the Professional Golfers' Association and the American PGA, sponsor Brian Park, the referee, the observers, the scorers, the British players Platts and Butler, and the four caddies. Where were the Americans, Boros and Lema? Byron Nelson moved through the spectators to call his men from the practice putting green, and Boros and Lema glided into the circle as the club clock showed 8.32. Now it was the turn of one of the official starters, in a box above the teeing-ground, to announce the players and quote their records. Then: 'On the tee, Julius Boros,' and the great match was alive.

Those who went with that first match had a horribly disappointing half-hour, for Platts and Butler started 5, 5, 5, against the Americans' 4, 4, 4, and already there were visions of a big American win which might set the pattern for the day. On the other hand the spectators who went off with our big men Thomas and Will against Marr and Palmer were soon in good heart, for long-driving Thomas and his broad-shouldered Scottish partner began 4, 3, 3—all birdies— against 5, 4, 4. The fortunes of the day and the hopes and fears of the

36

spectators were to seesaw in that way throughout the sunlit hours, but so much was to happen before the last stroke of the day—a 20-yard putt by Bernard Hunt which went down at the sixteenth hole to halve the series. Let us get back to the most encouraging sight for British eyes—Thomas and Will continuing their all-out attack on Palmer and Marr. It was Thomas who dominated the proceedings and some of his strokes were tremendous. With Marr pulling the first of several bad shots into a bunker at the first hole Thomas hit a great No. 4 iron shot over the hill to the green. He holed from four yards for a three at the second and Will, inspired by these perform-ances, confidently rolled in a six-yarder for a three at the third. Marr, right out of form, played a poor pitch to the 5th which went over the green, and sent a bunker shot over the green at the seventh where the British pair, also bunkered, were allowed to win in four, to become five up. They turned with that advantage, having done the nine holes in 33 strokes, and nothing the Americans could do would turn the tide. At the 13th (517 yards) Thomas hit a magnificent wooden club second shot to the edge of the green, and with that birdie four his side won by 6 and 5.

So far, so good, for O'Connor and Alliss, a wonderful pair, seemed to be getting the measure of Venturi and January, Coles and Hunt had recovered from a weak start to be still in the picture with Caspar and Littler, and Platts and Butler were performing prodigies on the putting greens in their efforts to retrieve their disastrous start. Platts had begun the recovery by holing for a two at the short 4th, and when this chunky newcomer to the British team sank a four-yarder for a birdie four at the 17th, to make his side only one down, the home pair had had only 25 putts. Would they get another one in on the home green to square the match? Boros's spoon shot to the eighteenth finished ten yards short of the green. Butler, with the whole green to aim at, pushed out his shot into a bunker and there was a groan from the enormous crowd around the green. Platts recovered well, the ball running 12 feet past the hole and there were wild cheers when Butler, keen to make amends, holed out for a four. But Lema had played a good chip and Boros, monumentally calm, put in the American ball from eight feet to halve the hole in four and win the match.

While all this drama was being enacted beneath the clubhouse windows O'Connor and Alliss were walking in from the fourteenth green, feeling well pleased with themselves, having taken full advan-tage of the indifferent form of Venturi and January, to win their match by five and four. The British pair had had matters mostly their own way from the very first hole, where Venturi pulled his drive into the 'Jutland' sandhill and the Americans took three to reach the green. Alliss missed a very short putt at the second but made amends for that slip by sinking a four-yarder for a birdie three at the third and a three-yarder for a two at the 4th. With three birdies in four holes the home players were already in command of the match, and although Alliss missed another tiddler at the fifth he and O'Connor halved the hole and kept their precious lead to the turn, which they reached in 33—a magnificent performance. The Americans added to their troubles by taking three putts at the eleventh to become three down and the end drew near when Venturi, desperately trying to match Alliss's power driving, pulled into a ditch. He had to pay a penalty stroke, and the British pair's par five was good enough to increase their lead to four. O'Connor was bunkered from the tee at the 14th and Alliss sent his recovery shot twelve yards past the hole, but the Irishman, who had played with great determination throughout, rammed in the long putt for a three. January made the green from the tee but Venturi putted five feet short and his partner missed, to give Britain victory by five and four.

We had great hopes that Coles and Hunt would prove to be a valuable partnership, and they were to have their measure of success later. But on this first morning against Casper and Littler things went wrong for them. Coles, a deliberate, painstaking player, usually takes some time to get going and this morning was no exception. The match had a disappointing start, because the Americans played three bad shots through the green and yet secured a half in five. Two fine strokes had carried the Britons to within a few feet of the green but Coles's chip from thickish grass just lacked the necessary steam and Hunt's putt of five feet for the hole ran round the edge. The Americans were again outplayed through the green at the second and this time paid the penalty, but they pulled themselves together and won four of the next six holes to get a grip on the game. Their recovery began at the short fourth where Casper holed a beautiful putt of eight yards for a birdie two. Coles missed his second shot to the difficult long sixth and put his teeshot into a bunker at the seventh. He made very few errors for the rest of the week but these had cost his side dear and when Littler hit a magnificent second to within eight feet of the pin at the eighth and his partner holed the putt for a three, things looked really black for Britain. But Littler hooked into a bad spot at the ninth and his side took three putts at the 12th to revive home hopes. It was only a momentary gleam. The

able Casper, who had missed few chances on the green, rolled in
another long putt for a birdie four at the long 15th and two halves
gave the Americans victory by 2 and 1.

It may be imagined with what elated feelings Thomas and Will
once more faced Palmer and Marr in the second round. The sun
shone on friend and foe alike and there was no hint of thunder in
the air, but a storm was about to break over the heads of the British
pair. It all began well enough, with Will outdriving Palmer at the
first hole and both sides getting in single putts for a half in four. But
then the avalanche. Marr, who had been the weakness of the
American partnership in the morning, was now on his best behaviour
and he rolled in a nine-yard putt for a birdie three on the second
green to give his side the lead. That started it. Palmer holed from
eight yards at the third and, after a half in three at the short fourth,
the great American almost holed his pitch for a two at the fifth.
Palmer was now a man inspired. He holed another great putt of
about eight yards at the sixth, and when the short seventh was
halved in threes the Americans had had six threes in a row. By the
turn the Britons, who had gone out in a one-under-par 34 with no
mistake, were four down to the Americans' 30—an incredible score
on this tremendous links, even allowing for the calm, easy conditions.
The boot was on the other foot with a vengeance, and how sweet
revenge must have tasted when Palmer and Marr, having reached
the green at the thirteenth with a drive and No. 4 iron and (of
course) sinking their putt for an eagle three, found themselves winners
at the very hole where, four hours earlier, they had suffered defeat
by the same opponents. Will and Thomas, who had not lost a hole
in the morning, were without a win in this match. They had ruffled
the eagle's feathers and had now felt the talons. It was poor con-
solation for them that their own score was only two strokes worse than
that of the earlier round.

The dramatic come-back of Palmer and Marr tended to over-
shadow an equally meritorious performance by Alliss and O'Connor,
who were proving a wonderful partnership, and got the better of
Casper and Littler after a great fight on the outward half. The
Americans had twos at both short holes, but Alliss and O'Connor,
with a birdie four at the eighth and a birdie three at the ninth,
reached the turn in 31 against 32 to lead by one hole. This was great
stuff which added to the afternoon riot of low scoring, and the
gallery, soon swelled to mammoth proportions by the ending of the
top match, saw some more brilliant exchanges on the way home.
The Americans had a great four at the long thirteenth to square the

match, after O'Connor had lipped the hole from three yards; and they very nearly took the lead at the 14th. But Alliss played a beautiful chip, and O'Connor, gratefully holing his short putt for a half, holed from seven yards on the next green to give Britain the lead again.

With the match so critically poised it was no time to invoke rules, but referee Binnie Clark had to be called on for a decision when the British ball at the 16th was found in long grass almost touching a plaque let into the side of the fairway and commemorating Arnold Palmer's great stroke from that point in the 1961 Open Championship. The rules allowed Alliss a free drop behind and clear of the 'immovable obstruction', and it was just the luck of the game that his new lie was better than the old one. He made no mistake with his iron shot to the green to get a half, and followed up this telling stroke by chipping dead at the 17th for a birdie four, the hole and the match. The winners, who had completed a notable double for Britain, were six under par for the seventeen holes, a performance in every way comparable with that of Palmer and Marr.

Meanwhile the third match had gone steadily and remorselessly in favour of Boros and Lema, who beat Martin and Hitchcock by five and four with a score three better than par. Under such conditions this was not an exceptional performance and the British players did nothing to justify the action of their captain in substituting them for Butler and Platts. It is true that Butler and Platts had lost their morning match but they had made a great recovery from a seemingly impossible situation and were full of steam after taking Boros and Littler to the home green. Perseverance with them might have paid better. But the decision had been made and we now looked to Coles and Hunt to level the scores on the day. We did not look in vain. Coles, now thoroughly warmed up, was a reformed character, and the opponents gave him and Hunt all the encouragement they needed at the start. The Americans were bunkered in two at the first hole. January quick-hooked into the jungle of willow scrub at the second, and Venturi topped his drive only 20 yards off the third tee. They saved the second with a good putt but lost the other two, and Hunt and Coles, playing perfect golf, went out in 34 to turn one up. Hunt put down a nine-yard putt for a three to win the tenth and at the eleventh Coles played a magnificent recovery stroke which had a considerable psychological effect. He had to squat in the middle of a gorse bush to play the ball, but got it out to within two feet of the hole for a hard half. The

British pair were still two up going to the 16th and there Hunt ran down a tremendous putt of fully 20 yards for a birdie three and the match by three and two.

It was the last stroke of a wonderful day. And no one in the British camp was grumbling.

7 Photo-Finish and Faded Hopes

As the sun climbed into the clear autumn sky on the second day the British hopes soared, but it was a photo-finish in the gathering dusk which gave America an invaluable lead of two points on the fourball series.

It was, unfortunately, an all-too-familiar picture. The Americans under pressure always seem to pull out their most telling strokes, and for Britain it was once more a case of so near and yet so far. The bare facts speak for themselves. Alliss and O'Connor, slipping from their dominating form of the previous day, lost to Marr and Palmer 5 and 4, and the other seven games all went to the home hole, where the cupholders won three, lost two, and halved two. So it was five–three on the day, nine–seven on the match so far; and, as the headlights swept and blinked over the vast acreage of the car park and the neighbouring roads streamed with 14,000 spectators on their way home, we felt that a great chance had been missed.

And what a chance it had been! Thomas and Will four up at the tenth and losing. Platts and Butler dormy four and only halving the match. Britain at one time heading for a 3–1 morning lead and in the end losing 1½–2½. The cup of disappointment was filling, and it overflowed in the afternoon when, after the home players had been leading in all four games, they again salvaged only 1½ points. Of course it was only a matter of a putt or two. If we had holed once or twice and the Americans had missed the picture would have been different. But that is often the case in these affairs—and it nearly always seems to be the Americans who hole the vital ones. One important factor, and one not to be lightly dismissed, is that the Americans are conditioned to fourball play, and temperamentally tuned to a time-consuming form of golf which is peculiarly unsuited to a championship links on a cold autumn day. The interminable lifting and marking of the balls, the waiting for various shots, and the difficulty of making out exactly what was happening, were endured by the enormous crowds and had to be endured because after all this was part of the Ryder Cup match and our men were fighting to win back that golden trophy. But two rounds of fourball games were more than enough for everyone on our side, and even if we had won the day no one would have regretted the passing of it and the return to the sanity of two-ball matches.

But it is time to return to the sad story of the day. No sadness at the start. Instead glee among the spectators as Britain's prospects grew rosier with every hole played. Thomas and Will dovetailed in true fourball fashion in the opening game against January and Jacobs and, out in 33, turned three up. Thomas got a great three at the tenth to make it four and they were still in that happy position with seven to go. Good enough? No. Not in a fourball match against Americans. The tide was stemmed at the 11th when January holed from three yards to save his side from being five down, and it ebbed steadily against our men from that point. The British players both took fours at both short holes—no dovetailing there—and the Americans, scoring three successive birdies, became almost incredibly dormy one. January holed a five-yarder at the 15th and two equally good putts by Jacobs at the 16th and 17th put America in the lead. And although neither Jacobs nor January could do better than a five at the home hole the British pair were equally unsuccessful. Cold douche No. 1.

The collapse of Platts and Butler was even more tragic and incomprehensible. They had started the day full of vim—4, 3, 3—and those birdies made them three up before the sun had dispersed the early-morning clouds. Butler rubbed it in by holing for a two at the seventh and although Casper birdied the eighth the home players were out in 33 and turned three up. Platts so far had not contributed to the British birdies but he notched one for himself at the tenth and Britain went on to become dormy four. Then the tragic, fatal mistake. Butler, with two for the match at the 15th after covering the 536 yards with two magnificent wooden club shots, took three putts. The Americans jumped in to win with a birdie four and had three more birdies in succession to halve the match. Littler holed single putts on the 16th and 17th greens and completed his mission by pitching dead for a four at the 18th.

Cold douche No. 2.

By this time O'Connor and Alliss, playing somewhat below their great form of the first day, possibly due in some measure to the fact that the Irishman was suffering from a cold, had lost to a four-under-par performance by Marr and Palmer, and we were left to hope that Coles and Hunt would save something from the wreck, by beating Boros and Lema. They did so, thank heaven, but here again it was a desperately near thing. A half in eagle threes at the first hole set the pattern for this, the greatest match of the morning, and each side was out in 32 and all square. Hunt, who had not then won a hole, did so at the tenth with a birdie three, and this slender lead was held all the way home. The Americans tried desperately to square, and Lema nearly did so with a fine pitch which finished stone dead at the 18th. But Hunt, to everyone's relief, holed his short putt for a four and victory.

It was impossible to forget entirely the disappointments of the morning, but the sheer excitement of the afternoon transcended all that had gone before. Alliss and O'Connor, out for revenge against Marr and Palmer, performed valiantly. They were out in 34, including a two at the 7th where O'Connor holed from six yards to turn one up. Two telling holes were the 11th, where O'Connor holed from four yards for a three, and the 12th, where Alliss, faced by a difficult borrow, holed from the edge of the green for a two. The crucial hole was the seventeenth where O'Connor missed a putt of three yards for a birdie four. Palmer had a seven-footer to square the match but he missed it, and in the early-evening mist Alliss hit the shot of the match, a wood second which finished eight feet from the hole. The Americans were short in two and Marr almost holed his pitch. But that was not good enough and the Americans conceded the match without asking Alliss to putt.

This was our greatest hour, but was to be our last full point of the day. Thomas and Will held January and Jacobs for a long time—to the turn, in fact, with both sides out in 35. But the Americans started home 3, 3, 3, winning the tenth and eleventh. Thomas, always at his best at the long holes, got a grand four at the fifteenth to reduce the gap to one, and they took the match to the home green where January holed from five yards for the half and the match.

Then came Platts and Butler, telling the same sad story of a lead built up against the same opponents, and a lead fritted away. The home players had four threes in a row against Casper and Littler to go out in 33 and turn two up, but a two by Casper at the 12th and a fine four by the same player at the fifteenth squared the game. They were still all even going to the last hole where Platts got a splendid birdie four after being bunkered from the tee. But Casper, who had also been trapped, had a three-yard putt for a halved hole and a halved match—and down it went.

And now for Coles and Hunt. Having, like the others, let an early lead slip away, could they recover and beat Lema and Venturi and square the whole contest? The British players had made a joyous outward half of 33 with a two by Coles at the fourth and a two by Hunt at the seventh. They turned two up and all seemed delightful. Then, in this match as in the others, the Americans struck back. Lema holed for a three at the tenth and for another three at the eleventh. Match square. Two holes later Lema was at it again. This time a four-yard putt went in for a two at the fourteenth to give America the lead and Coles and Hunt, try as they would, could do no more than halve the last four holes.

So Black Friday came to an end, appropriately enough in the gloaming, with everyone pondering on what might have been, and wondering, somewhat fearfully, what Saturday might have in store.

8 So Near . . . And Yet So Far

The day itself dawned fair and grew lovely—a perfect day for playing golf and watching golf, with not too much wind and, when the morning clouds had drifted away, bright sunshine to temper the autumn nip in the air. Such comfortable conditions and the atmosphere of excitement did much to dispel the gloom of Black Friday, and the early exchanges gave a reasonable ground for hope that our men still had a chance of saving the day or at any rate taking the fight to the last putt. But this mood gave place to a depressive feeling as the leading matches began to go steadily against us. By lunchtime it was clear that only a miracle could stop that Cup going back across the Atlantic. And as the afternoon wore away 14,000 spectators realised ruefully that this was not going to be another 'Lindrick'.

It was unfortunate that Christie O'Connor's heavy cold, which had affected his play on the previous day, was too bad for him to take part in the first round of the singles; for Britain, two down with sixteen to play, needed her full strength, and O'Connor fit and well could have been counted on with some confidence. Harry Weetman kept the other Irishman, Jimmy Martin, on the sidelines and this meant a match for Hitchcock, who was placed No. 1 in the batting order. There is a theory widely held in some quarters that if you play your weakness against strength you gain an advantage. In other words, offer up a sacrifice to the opponents' best man and so enhance the chances of winning games lower down the list. That kind of strategy in the past has led to various complications, particularly when both captains are 'on the fiddle', and common sense suggests that there is only one way to arrange a team—put your best men at the top. On this very morning the British tail wagged, but of what use is a wagging tail if the first four games have gone to the other side?

So we could feel sympathy with Jimmy Hitchcock on two counts—he was up against the mighty Palmer, and the match started at the hangman's hour—8 a.m. Now what would we do if we were up against Arnold Palmer on a cold October morning when most sensible people are having breakfast, and Palmer starts with a six? We'd take a six as well and let him off the hook. Which is precisely what Hitchcock did. Somehow those two figures on the *Daily Express* scoreboard—the first of the day—had an ominous look for

Britain. Hitchcock, it must be recorded, settled down to play some fine golf after that horrible experience—but Palmer had done with sixes. Hitchcock, two down after five holes, won the sixth and seventh with birdies to square. Later, when three down, he won the 12th and 13th to keep in the match. But Palmer birdied the 15th and 16th and that was that, the American, even with his six, being four under fours for the game.

That set the pattern for some time, with our men trying hard but seeing their opponents unleash telling blows at the critical moment. Platts was only one down to an outward half of 34 by the majestic, easy-to-watch Boros; and the Englishman, squaring with a fine birdie three at the doglegged tenth, was still very much alive five holes from home. Then Boros shot three birdies in a row and America had notched another point. Everyone who saw Boros, at 45 the oldest of an older-than-average United States team, marvelled at the deceptive ease of his long, lazy swing and his charming, gentle manner. A chunky man with a wide face on which a smile was always ready to appear, he did everything required of him efficiently, yet with an approach which to the stranger might have appeared almost casual.

Another whom everyone liked to watch was Tony Lema, who had made a noble and almost successful defence of his title in the Open Championship at Birkdale a few months earlier and on this last day of the Ryder Cup was to dazzle us with two fine performances. In this morning match against Butler, who was still without a win, the American went out in 33 to turn two up. Butler is a great fighter and when he drew level with a beautiful downhill putt at the sixteenth he seemed still to have a chance. But his second shots had been the weakest part of his game so far, and when he faded one into a bunker at the 18th it meant the end of his brave effort. He was deep in the hazard, it was impossible to reach the green with his recovery, and Lema's par five was good enough.

It seemed that nothing we could do could stand against these Americans and their powers of recovery. There is no doubt at all that Birkdale's great finish was proving a handicap to our side because the Americans were so very good at getting down in two from 50 or 60 yards. They were always that little bit more likely than our chaps to turn those par fives into birdie fours. Yet this was not so in the match between Coles and Marr, for the Englishman, having been two up at the fourth and losing four of the next five holes, made a spirited counter-attack over the last few holes. Marr took a six at the fifteenth and picked up at the 17th after being in trouble.

But in between he had got a four against Coles's five at the par four 16th, and Coles could do no better than a half in five at the eighteenth. So four games had gone to America, and some morale-boosting information was sadly needed in the British camp. It came in news of the progress of our two strong men, Hunt and Alliss. In Hunt we had a player who had the confidence, the courage and the skill to play the Americans at their own game, for no one in the other side side was his superior at holing the critical putts. Here he was, on this October morning, in a devil of a tussle with the pale, solemn-faced Gene Littler, who, both as a Walker Cup amateur and a Ryder Cup professional, had a wealth of experience behind him. Hunt was out in a par 35 and all square but he took the short 12th in three and kept his slender lead at the 14th by holing from fully ten yards for a birdie two, knowing that Littler (as he did) would hole his six-footer for a half. But Littler had one of his few wild drives at the fifteenth and, although winning back the sixteenth, was well beaten at the home hole, where Hunt hit a perfect approach shot and, with great smoothness and not a hint of nerves, put down his five-footer for a birdie four and the match.

David Thomas had by this time lost to Jacobs—lost tragically, for after going out in 34 to lead by two holes he had a terrible time on the way home. It all began at the tenth, where he was in trouble and picked up. Then came a six at the thirteenth and he lost a ball from another wild shot into the willow scrub at the fifteenth. Jacobs was now two up and two halves gave him the match. We were now in dire straits and could afford no more defeats. Fortunately the rest of the tail wagged to some purpose. First Alliss in what must be regarded as one of the finest matches of the week, certainly the best of the day. This powerful well-equipped Englishman seemed to have found that rare gift, consistency, which has eluded him for so long, and has seldom been more cheerfully sure of himself as he was against Casper on this sunny, exhilarating October morning. And in Casper he certainly had a worthy opponent. Each had only 13 putts in the first nine holes and Casper was out in 33. But he was one down to Alliss, who had done those nine holes in 32. Casper squared with a birdie at the 11th but he made rather a mess of the long 13th where Alliss had a majestic birdie four to regain the lead, and they slugged away at each other to halve the remaining five holes. Each could say that he had a foeman worthy of his steel, but we were immeasurably relieved to see Alliss win a game which either could have won without discrediting the other. And the picture we shall always carry in our minds is that of Alliss facing a putt of five feet for

victory on the home green after Casper had holed a good one of
nine feet for a birdie four. Did Alliss's mind go back to that Ryder
Cup match of 1953 when he had that kind of putt to halve with
Joe Turnesa and save the day for Britain? We do not know. We
only know that on this occasion Alliss was perfectly in control of
himself and the situation. With the greatest calmness he asked the
referee to decide whether a depression in front of his ball was or was
not a pitch mark. And on the verdict being given in his favour he
did a careful repair job, shaped up to the putt with his new and
successful left-hand-below-right putting grip, and knocked that ball
straight into the hole.

Mr. Harold Wilson, who had just arrived with the Earl of Derby,
President of the PGA, was in time to watch that great finish, and
immediately afterwards he saw George Will salvage half a point for
Britain by beating January all ends up with a birdie four against a
six at the 18th. Will had been two down with seven to play but got
back into the fight with twos at the 12th and 13th and was resolution
itself when it came to the sticking-point.

Such heroics immensely pleased the spectators now streaming
away for lunch, but the stark fact was that the Americans had added
three points to their overnight lead and now needed only two of the
eight remaining singles to win the Cup once more.

The long, sunny but rather cold afternoon was not half over when
the United States found themselves half-way to their goal, as a
result of some brilliant golf by Lema. Thomas's distressing experience
of the first round had convinced the burly, powerful Welshman that
he could do more good for his side by standing down than by playing
in the afternoon. Weetman had to choose between the two Irishmen
—O'Connor with a cold and Martin, who had shown indifferent
form in his only appearance of the week. O'Connor it had to be,
but in the event it would have mattered not one jot. O'Connor
played well, much better than we had any reason to expect in the
circumstances, and he was in fact one under fours for 14 holes. But
there were no more holes to play for Lema was eight under fours for
the same stretch and won by six and four. The American went out
in 33 to turn three up and then did 3, 3, 2, 5, 2—a devastating run
which would have been too much for anyone else on either side.

The positions in the other games provided an overall picture not
without comfort for the home camp. Butler, in the top match, had
been doing well at the expense of Palmer, who was in subdued mood
and, with an outward score of 37, turned one down. But the Englishman nodded at the two short holes coming home, Palmer in

D

between got a typically powerful birdie four at the long thirteenth, and all in a moment, it seemed, Butler was struggling. When he missed a putt of ten feet for a win at the seventeenth America were assured of keeping the Cup, and it remained to be seen whether Boros, then one up on Hitchcock playing the seventeenth, or Palmer would be the first to win the day for America. It was in a sense a dead-heat between these two great players, as the distant applause for Boros's win in five at the 17th was drowned in a great roar from thousands of spectators around the home green. For Palmer, with the 18th pin so much behind the left-hand bunker that it was considered impossible to get anywhere near the hole in two, even if it were physically possible to cover the necessary distance, not only hit a No. 3 wood all the way, but with such precision as to the amount of draw on it that the ball skirted the bunker and ran up to within four feet of the pin. It was a great stroke, fully deserving to be accorded the distinction of having won the match for America.

What followed was inevitably of academic interest, but it is pleasant to record that the British tail wagged again, largely because Alliss and Coles were playing lower than they should have done in the batting order. Alliss's win was at the expense of Venturi, who shared in some fine golf but was outplayed on the long finishing holes. The American had to pick up at the 517-yard 13th and Alliss, the real strong man with no hint of faltering, got birdie fours to win the 15th and 17th. So he finished the week with five points out of his six matches, as fine a performance as any British player has done in the long history of these contests. Coles, who seems to be a slow starter but a good finisher, had much the better of matters against Casper; and Platts, who had thus far performed doggedly without any luck, scored his first and only win of the week by getting the better of a dog fight with Jacobs. But Hunt, taking 75 for his last round, went down on the home green to Marr, and Will disappointingly lost to Littler after being gratuitously two up at the second hole. While playing the third Littler discovered that a No. 7 iron belonging to Don January was in his bag, making his armoury one more than the legal maximum of 14 clubs. Someone, probably a caddie, had made a mistake during the interval and dropped a club into the wrong bag, but however it had happened, the rules stipulate a penalty of two holes for such an infringement, even if the luckless player has gained no advantage. Will, understandably, was most reluctant to accept the situation. He would much prefer to have gone on all square, as the figures made it. But the referee had no option but to apply the rule, and by this means Will was able to turn one up with a score of 35. He was still in the lead four holes from home, but he made a mess of the 15th and 17th holes and Littler, having birdied the 16th, won by 2 and 1 to complete a sad day for Britain.

Mr. Wilson, participating unwillingly no doubt in this particular addition to the export drive, presented the Cup to smiling Byron Nelson, who had been so wonderful a captain. The British players put the best face possible on the situation, the spectators cheered everyone, the cars started streaming away, the organisers and their labour force were left to clear up, and a great week was over. It had been a wonderful week in every way, and while admiring the Americans for their sustained power and fine play under pressure, we all had the same thought. It could have been the other way round, and next time, perhaps, it will be.

9 In Retrospect

We have described the golf as it was played in those three hectic days in the October sunshine. In this chapter, with the advantage of hindsight, our task is to sum up the match, to bring out some of the highlights, and to probe into the shadows. For the picture, for British eyes, as we all know now, was not to be a brightly coloured 'Victory 1965', but a chiaroscuro in which good mingled with bad and hopes struggled with fears. If we had to select one scene for this drama enacted over the sandhills of Birkdale we would pick the 18th hole and its surroundings, for it was there that just half of the 32 games finished, and of those 16 which went the full distance Great Britain won five and halved three, the other eight going to America. In issues so close as this, with the difference between victory and defeat measured by the turn of a ball or the bending of a blade of grass, there can be no doubt that, as Byron Nelson admitted after the match, the margin of seven points in favour of his team bore no relation to the closeness of the match. Rarely, indeed, have the fortunes of two teams fluctuated so narrowly as they did in this 1965 Ryder Cup match, in which the sides were level at the end of the first day, and the Americans gradually drew away to win by 19½ points to 12½. Our rider to the verdict of Byron Nelson is that if there was little to choose between the teams the Americans won because they more often holed the decisive putt when under pressure. It is not a new observation. But if we go on record as stating that the result of the Ryder Cup match of 1965 depended on whether or not half a dozen putts finished in or out of the hole, none would gainsay us.

Nevertheless, peering once more into the shadows of our picture, we can see two of those 18th-green finishes on Friday morning which should never have been, and which dealt our cause a blow from which it never recovered. In one of these fourball games January and Jacobs of the United States beat Thomas and Will by one hole after having been four down with seven holes to play. In the other Platts and Butler of Great Britain only halved with Casper and Littler after having been dormy four. The United States finished that day leading by two points. If the home side had won those two games they would have gone into the last day's singles leading by one point. And who can say to what extent that would have stimulated our chances on the Saturday? Who can assess the psychological impact of a lead against a deficit? We can only point to those two setbacks as the most sombre chapters in our tale of what might have been.

It is easy to be wise after the event and say that Butler, having hit two magnificent woods to the long and desperately testing 15th, and having two putts for a birdie four and the match, should never have putted past the hole and so given himself a downhill return. But these things happen, and if locker-room echoes could speak they would resound with comments beginning 'If only . . .' and 'But for . . .'.

As at all inquests of this kind many reasons can be advanced for what happened. Some of these are hoary with age. America is a much larger country and therefore can call on many more players of Ryder Cup calibre. Americans are accustomed to more or less similar playing conditions all the year round, whereas our players are constantly having to improvise. Americans have much more and much keener competitions, are subject to tournament pressures for 50 weeks in every year, and no occasion is more important than another. And so on. Some of these arguments might have been valid years ago when all our Ryder Cup men had club jobs, played in no more than half a dozen events a year and rarely went abroad. But we used to win the Ryder Cup in those days—at any rate in this country—and now we lose consistently on both sides of the Atlantic, when such alibis can no longer be offered. Nevertheless the Americans do play more tournament golf and have greater incentives. At the dinner given by the PGA after the match at Southport Byron Nelson said of his team that the ten men between them had won no fewer than 145 tournaments to date and collected a total of more than 4 million dollars in prize money. The biggest share had gone to Arnold Palmer, but if the American professionals cannot all be Palmers they all try like the devil to be Palmers, and in the process become almost automatons of the links.

The 1965 match was so close that if the Americans had missed half a dozen putts that they holed and the British had holed half a dozen that they missed the result might well have been reversed. But that does not quite hit the target. Byron Nelson, talking to us after the match, put his finger on the spot by saying the only real advantage held by his team was in the playing of pitch shots of 60 yards and under. They got the ball nearer to the hole from such strokes and therefore made the putting easier.

This superiority of the Americans was most marked at the long par-five holes and accounted in large measure for the fact that in several matches the home players flattered only to deceive. When neither side could get up in two the pitch into the green carried a premium far higher than that on any other stroke in the game. Of course this is no newly discovered truth. 'Running three shots into two' has been the stock-in-trade of American golfers since Walter Hagen's day.

Well, there it is. Britain tried hard and lost. The golf on both sides was at times magnificent, usually competent and rarely indifferent. There was little to choose between two fine teams; spectators, totalling nearly 50,000 for the three days, had a wonderful feast of golf; the organisation was perfect and the weather all that could be desired. And there need be no recriminations. We stand again at that 18th hole on that Saturday afternoon and see Arnold Palmer's ball from a No. 3 wood sail through the air, swerve round the bunker and roll to four feet from the hole, and say once more in our hearts that the man who could play a shot like that deserves everything that fortune can give him. That stroke, which settled the Ryder Cup match, pinpointed the reason for the Americans' triumph. When the master stroke was demanded it was usually an American who played it.

The Ryder Cup 1965

Royal Birkdale Golf Club, Southport, Lancs. October 7, 8 and 9

Great Britain		U.S.A.	
FOURSOMES: MORNING			
L. Platts and P. J. Butler ..	o	J. Boros and A. Lema (1 hole)	1
D. J. Thomas and G. Will (6		A. Palmer and D. Marr ..	o
and 5)	1	W. Casper and G. Littler (2	
B. J. Hunt and N. C. Coles..	o	and 1)	1
P. Alliss and C. O'Connor (5		K. Venturi and D. January..	o
and 4)	1		—
	—		2
	2		
FOURSOMES: AFTERNOON			
D. J. Thomas and G. Will ..	o	A. Palmer and D. Marr (6 and	
P. Alliss and C. O'Connor (2		5	1
and 1)	1	W. Casper and G. Littler ..	o
J. Martin and J. Hitchcock ..	o	J. Boros and A. Lema (5 and 4)	1
B. J. Hunt and N. C. Coles (3		K. Venturi and D. January..	o
and 2)	1		—
	—		2
	2		
FOURBALL MATCHES: MORNING			
D. J. Thomas and G. Will ..	o	D. January and T. Jacobs	
L. Platts and P. J. Butler		(1 hole)	1
(halved)	½	W. Casper and G. Littler	
P. Alliss and C. O'Connor ..	o	(halved)	½
N. C. Coles and B. J. Hunt		D. Marr and A. Palmer	
(1 hole)	1	(5 and 4)	1
	—	J. Boros and A. Lema ..	o
	1½		—
			2½

FOURBALL: AFTERNOON

P. Alliss and C. O'Connor (1 hole)	1	D. Marr and A. Palmer .. 0
D. Thomas and G. Will ..	0	D. January and T. Jacobs (1 hole) 1
L. Platts and P. J. Butler (halved)	½	W. Casper and G. Littler (halved) .. .. .. ½
B. J. Hunt and N. C. Coles..	0	A. Lema and K. Venturi (1 hole) 1

$$1\tfrac{1}{2}$$

$$2\tfrac{1}{2}$$

SINGLES: MORNING

J. Hitchcock	0	A. Palmer (3 and 2).. ..	1
L. Platts	0	J. Boros (4 and 2)	1
P. J. Butler	0	A. Lema (1 hole)	1
N. C. Coles	0	D. Marr (2 holes)	1
B. J. Hunt (2 holes)	1	G. Littler	0
P. Alliss (1 hole)	1	W. Casper	0
D. J. Thomas..	0	T. Jacobs (2 and 1)	1
G. Will (halved)	½	D. January (halved).. ..	½

$$2\tfrac{1}{2}$$

$$5\tfrac{1}{2}$$

SINGLES: AFTERNOON

P. J. Butler	0	A. Palmer (2 holes)	1
J. Hitchcock	0	J. Boros (2 and 1)	1
C. O'Connor	0	A. Lema (6 and 4)	1
P. Alliss (3 and 1)	1	K. Venturi	0
N. C. Coles (3 and 2) ..	1	W. Casper	0
G. Will	0	G. Littler (2 and 1)	1
B. J. Hunt	0	D. Marr (1 hole)	1
L. Platts (1 hole)	1	T. Jacobs	0

3

5

Grand Total: Great Britain 12½, U.S.A. 19½.

Captains: H. Weetman (non-playing), *Great Britain*, and B. Nelson (non-playing), *U.S.A.*

Hole by Hole Figures

FOURSOMES: MORNING

Thomas and Will (G.B.). Out:
4, 3, 3, 3, 4, 4, 4, 4, 4—33. In: 4,
4, 3, 4 (3 under par).
Marr and Palmer (U.S.). Out:
5, 4, 4, 3, 5, 4, 5, 4, 4—38. In: 4,
4, 5, 4 (5 over par).
Great Britain won, 6 and 5.

O'Connor and Alliss (G.B.).
Out: 4, 5, 3, 2, 4, 5, 3, 4, 4—34.
In: 4, 4, 3, 5, 3 (1 under par).
Venturi and January (U.S.).
Out: 5, 4, 5, 3, 4, 5, 3, 4, 4—37.
In: 4, 5, 3, 6, 4 (5 over par).
Great Britain won, 5 and 4.

Boros and Lema (U.S.). Out:
4, 4, 4, 3, 3, 4, 3, 4, 4—33. In: 4,
4, 3, 5, 3, 5, 4, 5, 4—37. Total: 70.
Platts and Butler (G.B.). Out:
5, 5, 5, 2, 3, 4, 3, 4, 4—35. In: 5,
4, 3, 4, 4, 4, 4, 4, 4—36. Total 71.:
United States won by one hole.

Casper and Little (U.S.). Out:
5, 5, 4, 2, 4, 4, 3, 3, 5—35. In: 4,
4, 4, 5, 3, 4, 4, 5 (level with par).
Hunt and Coles (G.B.). Out: 5,
4, 4, 3, 4, 5, 4, 4, 4—37. In: 4, 4,
3, 5, 3, 5, 4, 5 (2 over par).
United States won, 2 and 1.

FOURSOMES: AFTERNOON

Marr and Palmer (U.S.). Out:
4, 3, 3, 3, 3, 3, 3, 4, 4—30. In: 4,
4, 3, 3 (7 under par).
Thomas and Will (G.B.). Out:
4, 4, 4, 3, 4, 4, 3, 4, 4—34. In: 5,
4, 3, 5 (level with par).
United States won, 6 and 5.

O'Connor and Alliss (G.B.).
Out: 4, 4, 3, 3, 3, 4, 3, 4, 3—31.
In: 4, 4, 3, 5, 3, 4, 4, 4 (6 under par).
Casper and Littler (U.S.). Out:
4, 4, 4, 3, 2, 4, 2, 5, 4—32. In: 4,
4, 3, 4, 3, 5, 4, 5 (4 under par).
Great Britain won, 2 and 1.

Boros and Lema (U.S.). Out:
4, 4, 4, 2, 3, 5, 2, 4, 4—32. In: 4,
4, 3, 5, 3 (3 under par).
Martin and Hitchcock (G.B.).
Out: 4, 4, 5, 3, 4, 5, 2, 5, 4—36.
In: 4, 4, 3, 5, 4 (2 over par).
United States won, 5 and 4.

Hunt and Coles (G.B.). Out:
3, 4, 4, 3, 4, 4, 4, 4, 4—34. In: 3,
4, 3, 5, 3, 4, 3 (4 under par).
Venturi and January (U.S.).
Out: 5, 4, 7, 3, 3, 4, 3, 5, 4—38.
In: 4, 4, 3, 4, 4, 4, 4 (2 over par).
Great Britain won 3 and 2.

MATCH RESULT: Great Britain 4, U.S.A. 4.

FOURBALL MATCHES: MORNING

Marr and Palmer (U.S.). Out: 4, 4, 4, 3, 3, 4, 3, 4, 4—33. In: 3, 4, 3, 4, 3 (4 under par).
Alliss and O'Connor (G.B.). Out: 4, 4, 4, 3, 4, 5, 3, 5, 4—36. In: 4, 4, 3, 5, 3 (1 over par).
United States won, 5 and 4.

January and Jacobs (U.S.). Out: 5, 3, 4, 3, 4, 5, 3, 5, 4—36. In: 4, 4, 2, 4, 3, 4, 3, 4, 5—33. Total: 69.
Thomas and Will (G.B.). Out: 4, 3, 4, 3, 4, 4, 3, 4, 4—33. In: 3, 4, 4, 4, 4, 5, 4, 5, 5—38. Total: 71.
United States won by one hole.

Platts and Butler (G.B.). Out: 4, 4, 4, 3, 3, 3, 3, 5, 4—33. In: 4, 4, 3, 5, 3, 5, 3, 5, 4—36. Total: 69.
Casper and Littler (U.S.). Out: 4, 4, 5, 3, 3, 4, 3, 5, 4—35. In: 4, 4, 2, 5, 3, 4, 4, 4, 4—34. Total: 69.
Match halved.

Lema and Venturi (U.S.). Out: 4, 4, 4, 3, 4, 4, 3, 5, 4—35. In: 3, 3, 3, 5, 2, 4, 4, 5, 5—34. Total: 69.
Coles and Hunt (G.B.). Out: 4, 5, 4, 2, 3, 4, 2, 5, 4—33. In: 4, 4, 3, 5, 3, 4, 4, 5, 5—37. Total: 70.
United States won by one hole.

FOURBALL MATCHES: AFTERNOON

Alliss and O'Connor (G.B.). Out: 4, 4, 5, 3, 4, 4, 2, 5, 3—34. In: 4, 3, 2, 4, 3, 5, 4, 5, 3—34. Total: 68.
Marr and Palmer (U.S.). Out: 4, 4, 4, 3, 4, 5, 3, 4, 4—35. In: 3, 4, 3, 4, 3, 4, 4, 5, 4—34. Total: 69.
Great Britain won by one hole.

January and Jacobs (U.S.). Out: 5, 4, 4, 3, 3, 4, 3, 5, 4—35. In: 3, 3, 3, 4, 3, 5, 4, 5, 4—34. Total: 69.
Thomas and Will (G.B.). Out: 4, 4, 4, 3, 3, 4, 3, 6, 4—35. In: 4, 4, 3, 4, 3, 4, 4, 5, 4—35. Total: 70
United States won by one hole.

Platts and Butler (G.B.). Out: 4, 3, 3, 3, 4, 4, 2, 5, 4—32. In: 4, 3, 3, 5, 3, 5, 4, 5, 5—37. Total: 69.
Casper and Littler (U.S.). Out: 5, 4, 4, 3, 4, 4, 3, 4, 4—35. In: 4, 4, 3, 5, 3, 4, 3, 4, 4—34. Total: 69.
Match halved.

Coles and Hunt (G.B.). Out: 3, 4, 4, 3, 3, 4, 3, 4, 4—32. In: 3, 4, 3, 5, 3, 4, 4, 4, 4—34. Total: 66.
Boros and Lema (U.S.). Out: 3, 3, 4, 3, 4, 4, 3, 4, 4—32. In: 4, 4, 3, 5, 3, 4, 4, 4, 4—35. Total 67.
Great Britain won by one hole.

MATCH RESULT: Great Britain 2, U.S.A. 4 (2 halved).

SINGLES: MORNING

Palmer (U.S.). Out: 6, 4, 4, 3, 3, 4, 3, 3, 4—34. In: 3, 4, 4, 5, 3, 4, 3 (3 under par).
Hitchcock (G.B.). Out: 6, 4, 5, 3, 4, 3, 2, 4, 5—36. In: 3, 5, 3, 4, 3, 5, 4 (par).
U.S. won 3 and 2.

Boros (U.S.). Out: 5, 4, 4, 2, 4, 3, 3, 5, 4—34. In: 4, 4, 3, 5, 2, 4, 4 (2 under par).
Platts (G.B.). Out: 5, 4, 5, 2, 4, 3, 3, 5, 4—35. In: 3, 4, 4, 5, 4, 5, 5 (3 over par).
U.S. won 4 and 2.

Lema (U.S.). Out: 4, 4, 4, 2, 4, 4, 3, 4, 4—33. In: 5, 4, 3, 5, 3, 5, 4, 5, 5—39. Total: 72.
Butler (G.B.). Out: 5, 4, 4, 3, 3, 4, 3, 5, 4—35. In: 4, 4, 3, 5, 3, 5, 3, 5, 6—38. Total: 73.
U.S. won by 1 hole.

Marr (U.S.). Out: 5, 4, 4, 4, 4, 3, 3, 4, 3—34. In: 4, 4, 3, 5, 3, 6, 4, 6, 4—39. Total: 73.
Coles (G.B.). Out: 4, 4, 4, 3, 5, 4, 3, 5, 4—36. In: 4, 4, 3, 5, 3, 4, 5, 5, 5—38. Total: 74.
U.S. won by 2 holes.

Hunt (G.B.). Out: 5, 4, 4, 3, 4, 3, 2, 5, 4—34. In: 3, 4, 3, 5, 2, 4, 5, 5, 4—35. Total: 69.
Littler (U.S.). Out: 4, 4, 4, 3, 4, 3, 3, 5, 4—34. In: 3, 4, 4, 5, 2, 5, 4, 5, 5—37. Total: 71.
G.B. won by 2 holes.

Alliss (G.B.). Out: 4, 4, 4, 2, 3, 5, 3, 4, 3—32. In: 4, 4, 3, 4, 3, 5, 4, 5, 4—36. Total. 68.
Casper (U.S.). Out: 5, 4, 3, 3, 3, 4, 3, 4, 4—33. In: 4, 3, 3, 6, 3, 5, 4, 5, 4—37. Total: 70.
G.B. won by 1 hole.

Jacobs (U.S.). Out: 4, 5, 4, 3, 3, 5, 3, 5, 4—36. In: 3, 4, 3, 4, 3, 5, 4, 5 (1 under par).
Thomas (G.B.). Out: 4, 4, 4, 3, 4, 5, 2, 5, 3—34. In: 0, 4, 4, 6, 3, 0, 4, 5 (picked up at 2 holes).
U.S. won 2 and 1.

Will (G.B.). Out: 5, 4, 4, 3, 4, 5, 3, 5, 4—37. In: 4, 4, 2, 0, 2, 4, 4, 5, 4 (picked up at 1 hole).
January (U.S.). Out: 4, 4, 4, 4, 4, 4, 3, 5, 3—35. In: 5, 3, 3, 4, 3, 5, 3, 5, 6—37. Total: 72.
Match halved.

SINGLES: AFTERNOON

Palmer (U.S.). Out: 5, 4, 4, 3, 4, 4, 4, 4, 5—37. In: 4, 4, 3, 4, 3, 4, 5, 5, 3—35. Total: 72.
Butler (G.B.). Out: 5, 4, 4, 2, 3, 5, 4, 5, 4—36. In: 4, 4, 4, 5, 4, 4, 4, 5, 4—38. Total: 74.
U.S. won by 2 holes.

Boros (U.S.). Out: 4, 4, 3, 3, 4, 5, 3, 5, 4—35. In: 4, 4, 3, 4, 3, 5, 4, 5 (1 under par).
Hitchcock (G.B.). Out. 4, 4, 5, 3, 4, 4, 3, 4, 5—36. In: 4, 4, 3, 5, 3, 5, 4, 6 (2 over par).
U.S. won 2 and 1.

Lema (U.S.). Out: 4, 4, 3, 3, 4, 4, 2, 5, 4—33. In: 3, 3, 2, 5, 2 (6 under par).

O'Connor (G.B.). Out: 4, 5, 4, 4, 3, 4, 3, 5, 4—36. In: 3, 5, 3, 5, 3 (1 over par).

U.S. won 6 and 4.

Alliss (G.B.). Out: 4, 4, 4, 3, 4, 4, 3, 4, 4—34. In: 5, 4, 3, 5, 3, 4, 4, 4 (2 under par).

Venturi (U.S.). Out: 4, 3, 4, 3, 4, 4, 3, 5, 4—34. In: 5, 4, 3, 6, 3, 5, 4, 5 (1 over par).

G.B. won 3 and 1.

Marr (U.S.). Out: 4, 4, 5, 3, 3, 4, 3, 5, 5—36. In: 4, 4, 3, 5, 3, 5, 4, 5, 5—38. Total 74.

Hunt (G.B.). Out: 4, 4, 4, 4, 3, 5, 4, 4, 5—37. In: 3, 4, 3, 5, 4, 5, 3, 6, 5—38. Total: 75.

U.S. won by 1 hole.

Coles. (G.B.). Out: 5, 3, 5, 3, 4, 5, 2, 6, 4—37. In: 3, 4, 3, 5, 3, 5, 4 (1 over par).

Caspar (U.S.). Out: 4, 4, 5, 4, 4, 5, 3, 4, 4—37. In: 4, 4, 3, 5, 3, 6, 4 (3 over par).

G.B. won 3 and 2.

Littler (U.S.). Out: 4, 5, 3, 3, 5, 2, 4, 3,—34. (conceding 2 holes because of 15 clubs in bag). In: 4, 5, 3, 5, 3, 5, 3, 5.

Will (G.B.). Out: 4, 5, 4, 3, 4, 4, 3, 4, 4—35. In: 4, 4, 4, 5, 3, 6, 4, 6 (3 over par).

U.S. won by 2 and 1.

Platts (G.B.). Out: 5, 4, 4, 4, 4, 5, 3, 5, 4—38. In: 3, 4, 4, 6, 3, 4, 5, 4, 5—38. Total: 76.

Jacobs (U.S.). Out: 4, 4, 5, 3, 4, 5, 4, 6, 5—40. In: 4, 4, 3, 5, 3, 5, 4, 4, 5—37. Total: 77.

G.B. won by 1 hole.

MATCH RESULT: Great Britain 5½, U.S.A. 10½.

OVERALL RESULT: Great Britain 12½, U.S.A. 19½.

Individual records: American

NAME	YEARS	MATCHES			
		PLAYED	WON	LOST	HALVED
Skip Alexander	1949, 1951	2	1	1	
Jerry Barber	1955, 1961	5	1	4	
Herman Barron	1947	1	1	0	
Tommy Bolt	1955, 1957	4	3	1	
Julius Boros	1959, 1963, 1965	11	7	2	2
Billy Burke	1931, 1933	3	3	0	
Jack Burke, Jr.	1951, 1953, 1955, 1957, 1959	8	7	1	
Walter Burkemo	1953	1	0	1	
Bill Casper, Jr.	1961, 1963, 1965	14	7	3	4
Bill Collins	1961	3	1	2	
Wilfred Cox	1931	2	2	0	
Jimmy Demaret	**1941, 1947, 1949, 1951	6	6	0	
Leo Diegel	1927, 1929, 1931, 1933	6	3	3	
Dave Douglas	1953	2	1	0	1
Ed Dudley	1929, 1933, 1937	4	3	1	
Olin Dutra	1933, 1935	4	1	3	
Al Espinosa	1927, 1929, 1931	4	2	1	1
Johnny Farrell	1927, 1929, 1931	6	3	2	1
Dow Finsterwald	1957, 1959, 1961, 1963	13	9	3	1
Doug Ford	1955, 1957, 1959, 1961	9	4	4	1
Ed Furgol	1957	1	0	1	
Marty Furgol	1955	1	0	1	
Vic Ghezzi	*1939, **1941	0	0	0	
Bob Goalby	1963	5	3	1	1
Johnny Golden	1927, 1929	3	3	0	
Ralph Guldahl	1937, *1939	2	2	0	
Fred Haas, Jr.	1953	1	0	1	
Walter Hagen	1927, 1929, 1931, 1933, 1935	9	7	1	1
Bob Hamilton	1949	2	0	2	
M. R. (Chick) Harbert	1949, 1955	2	2	0	
Chandler Harper	1955	1	0	1	
E. J. (Dutch) Harrison	1947, 1949, 1951	3	2	1	
Fred Hawkins	1957	2	1	1	
Clayton Heafner	1949, 1951	4	3	0	1
Jay Hebert	1959, 1961	4	2	1	1

Lionel Hebert	1957	1	0	1	
Jimmy Hines	*1939	0	0	0	
Ben Hogan	**1941, 1947, 1951	3	3	0	
Tommy Jacobs	1965	4	3	1	
Don January	1965	5	2	2	1
Herman Keiser	1947	1	0	1	
Ted Kroll	1953, 1955, 1957	4	3	1	
Ky Laffoon	1935	1	0	1	
Tony Lema	1963, 1965	11	8	1	2
Gene Littler	1961, 1963, 1965	14	5	3	6
Harold McSpaden	*1939, **1941	0	0	0	
Lloyd Mangrum	**1941, 1947, 1949, 1951, 1953	8	6	2	
Dave Marr	1965	6	4	2	
Billy Maxwell	1963	4	4	0	
Dick Mayer	1957	2	1	0	1
William Mehlhorn	1927	2	1	1	
Tony Menero	1937	2	1	1	
Dick Metz	*1939	0	0	0	
Cary Middlecoff	1953, 1955, 1959	6	2	3	1
Byron Nelson	1937, *1939, **1941, 1947	4	3	1	
Ed Oliver	1947, 1951, 1953	5	3	2	
Arnold Palmer	1961, 1963, 1965	16	11	4	1
Johnny Palmer	1949	2	0	2	
Sam Parks, Jr.	1935	1	0	0	1
Henry Picard	1935, 1937, *1939	4	3	1	
Johnny Pott	1963, 1965	3	1	2	
Dave Ragan	1963	4	2	1	1
Henry Ransom	1951	1	0	1	
Johnny Revolta	1935, 1937	3	2	1	
Bob Rosburg	1959	2	2	0	
Paul Runyan	1933, 1935, *1939	4	2	2	
Gene Sarazen	1927, 1929, 1931, 1933, 1935, 1937, **1941	12	7	2	3
Denny Shute	1931, 1933, 1937	6	2	2	2
Horton Smith	1929, 1931, 1933, 1935, 1937, *1939, **1941	4	3	0	1
Sam Snead	1937, *1939, 1941, 1947, 1949, 1951, 1953, 1955, 1959	13	10	2	1
Mike Souchak	1959, 1961	6	5	1	
Jim Turnesa	1953	1	1	0	

Joe Turnesa	1927, 1929	4	1	2	1
Ken Venturi	1965	4	1	3	
Art Wall, Jr.	1957, 1959, 1961	6	4	2	
Al Watrous	1927, 1929	3	2	1	
Craig Wood	1931, 1933, 1935, **1941	4	1	3	
Lew Worsham	1947	2	2	0	

Individual records: British

NAME	YEARS	MATCHES			
		PLAYED	WON	LOST	HALVED
Jimmy Adams	1947, 1949, 1951, 1953	7	2	5	
Percy Alliss	1933, 1935, 1937	6	3	2	1
Peter Alliss	1953, 1957, 1959, 1961, 1963, 1965	13	7	6	
Laurie Ayton	1949	0	0	0	
Aubrey Boomer	1927, 1929	4	2	2	
Ken Bousfield	1949, 1951, 1957, 1959, 1961	10	5	5	
Harry Bradshaw	1953, 1955, 1957	5	2	2	1
Eric Brown	1953, 1955, 1957, 1959	8	4	4	
Dick Burton	1935, 1937, 1949	5	2	3	
Jack Busson	1935	2	0	2	
Peter Butler	1965	5	0	3	2
Neil Coles	1961, 1963 , 1965	16	5	8	3
Archie Compston	1927, 1929, 1931	6	1	4	1
Henry Cotton	1929, 1937, 1947	6	2	4	
Bill Cox	1935, 1937	3	0	2	1
Fred Daly	1947, 1949, 1951, 1953	8	3	4	1
William Davies	1931, 1933	4	2	2	
Norman Drew	1959	1	0	0	1
George Duncan	1927, 1929, 1931	5	2	3	
Syd Easterbrook	1931, 1933	3	2	1	
John Fallon	1955	1	1	0	
Max Faulkner	1947, 1949, 1951, 1953, 1957	8	1	7	
Eric Green	1947	0	0	0	
Tom Haliburton	1961, 1963	6	0	6	
Jack Hargreaves	1951	0	0	0	

Arthur Havers	1927, 1931, 1933	6	3	3	
Jimmy Hitchcock	1965	3	0	3	
Bert Hodson	1931	1	0	1	
Reg Horne	1947	0	0	0	
Brian Huggett	1963	5	2	2	1
Bernard Hunt	1953, 1957, 1959, 1961, 1963, 1965	21	6	12	3
Geoffrey Hunt	1963	3	0	3	
John Jacobs	1955	2	2	0	
Ted Jarman	1935	1	0	1	
Herbert Jolly	1927	2	0	2	
Sam King	1937, 1947, 1949	5	1	3	1
Arthur Lacey	1933, 1937	3	0	3	
Arthur Lees	1947, 1949, 1951, 1953	8	4	4	
Jimmy Martin	1965	1	0	1	
Peter Mills	1957	1	1	0	
Abe Mitchell	1929, 1931, 1933	6	4	2	
Ralph Moffitt	1961	1	0	1	
Christy O'Connor	1955, 1957, 1959, 1961, 1963, 1965	19	7	11	1
Alf Padgham	1933, 1935, 1937	6	0	6	
John Panton	1951, 1953, 1961	5	0	5	
Alf Perry	1933, 1935, 1937	4	0	3	1
Lionel Platts	1965	5	1	2	2
Ted Ray	1927	2	0	2	
Dai Rees	1937, 1947, 1949, 1951, 1953, 1955, 1957, 1959, 1961	18	7	10	1
Fred Robson	1927, 1929, 1931	6	2	4	
Syd Scott	1955	2	0	2	
Dave Thomas	1959, 1963, 1965	13	1	9	3
Charles Ward	1947, 1949, 1951	6	1	5	
Harry Weetman	1951, 1953, 1955, 1957, 1959, 1961, 1963	15	2	11	2
Charles Whitcombe	1927, 1929, 1931, 1933, 1935, 1937	9	3	2	4
Ernest Whitcombe	1929, 1931, 1935	6	1	4	1
Reginald Whitcombe	1935	1	0	1	
George Will	1963, 1965	5	1	2	2

* 1939 matches cancelled, because of World War II.
** 1941 matches not scheduled, because of World War II.

A Past Occasion

Mr. Samuel Ryder (sixth from left) at the XIX Club Dinner to the 1935 Ryder Cup team before departing for America. Players in the picture include Arthur Havers, Charles Whitcombe and Abe Mitchell.

JULIUS BOROS popped up quite unexpectedly from the ranks of the almost unknown to win the U.S. Open title at the age of 32. And when he won that title for the second time in 1963 he was already a veteran in terms of years. But Boros keeps on winning prize money and at 45 had the distinction of getting his third Ryder Cup cap.

BILLY CASPER at 34 can look back on a decade of rich rewards culminating in a 90,000-dollar return for his efforts in 1964. He was U.S. Open Champion in 1959 and a member of the U.S. Ryder Cup team at Lytham in 1961, when he won all his games.

TOMMY JACOBS, like so many others on the tough U.S. circuit, has had his lean years. But three years ago he shook off depression and started a good run which carried him into the Ryder Cup team for the first time. He finished second to Venturi in the U.S. Open of 1964 and since then has been with the leaders in most tournaments.

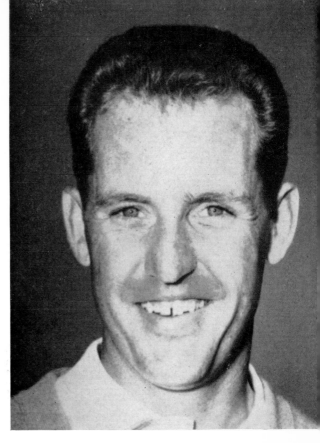

DON JANUARY is not only one of the most consistent U.S. golfers of the present time but also a powerful hitter of the ball, as becomes a tall, strongly built Texan. He hasn't had a bad year since turning pro in 1955, and in 1963 he won over 33,000 dollars, his biggest total if one excepts the 50,000 dollars he won for just one stroke—a hole in one at Palm Springs in 1961. Surprising to think that this 1965 affair was his first Ryder Cup match.

TONY LEMA, like Palmer, has become a familiar figure with British spectators. He won the Open at St. Andrews at the first attempt and after only one practice round on the Old Course, which he had never seen before. And, true to reputation, he regaled the Press with that cheerful drink which has given him the title of 'Champagne Tony'. A charming, modest-looking chap with nevertheless a glint in the eye which means business.

GENE LITTLER is the stylist of the U.S. team and one of its 'old timers'. He won the U.S. Amateur Championship in 1953, playing in the Walker Cup match of that year, and soon afterwards turned pro. He won the U.S. Open Championship in 1961 and as champion played in the Ryder Cup match at Lytham, but only halved his singles with Coles and O'Connor.

DAVE MARR, a newcomer to Ryder Cup golf, crowned five years of steady development by winning the U.S. PGA Championship of 1965. He is slightly built but has a sound style and, even by American standards, is a good putter. He started collecting Ryder Cup points in 1964 when he touched his best form by finishing eleventh in the prize-money records.

ARNOLD PALMER has been so long the darling of galleries on both sides of the Atlantic that he has become an institution. His two Open Championship victories, his four U.S. Masters titles, his half-million dollars of prize money in ten years, rank him with Hagen, Hogan and Vardon as one of the greatest professional players of all time. The glamour persists—the biggest gallery at Birkdale, it seemed, was always 'Arnie's Army'.

JOHNNY POTT is a professional through and through, son of a pro and a member of the U.S. PGA Tournament Committee. As one of the youngest members of the U.S. team he made his first visit to Britain this year, but unluckily suffered an injury to a rib muscle which prevented him from playing. He has had his ups and downs but at 29 has still many years of good golf in front of him.

KEN VENTURI, after representing the United States in the Walker Cup matches, turned pro in 1954 and did very well for a time, but he then had a run of bad luck and a back injury threatened to put him out of the game in 1962. He recovered and in 1964 won the U.S. Open Championship, was made 'Player of the Year', and started amassing the points which gained him a Ryder Cup place.

BYRON NELSON was the first man to profit on a large scale in the golf prize-money boom of the 'thirties, and in a decade which included the war years he was three times top money winner on the U.S. circuit, twice U.S. Open Champion, twice Master Golfer and twice PGA champion. His career lasted only a decade because he found the strain too much and retired from regular tournament play in 1945, taking a farm in his native Texas. He played in the 1937 Ryder Cup match at Southport (losing to Dai Rees in the singles) and his return there as Captain of the U.S. side was very popular.

Captain Nelson and his crew

PETER ALLISS is the son of a Ryder Cup golfer and himself possesses a great record in the series, having not lost a singles match in the last four contests. He halved with Palmer at Lytham in 1961 and beat him at Atlanta, Georgia, in 1963. Alliss is one of the longest hitters in British professional golf, and it is one of the game's mysteries that he has not won much more often than the records show.

PETER BUTLER, always an earnest, painstaking performer, has brought patience and perseverance to the task of making himself a Ryder Cup golfer, and achieved his aim by being runner-up in the match-play championship of 1964 and the PGA championship of 1965 as well as securing two tournament victories. But his outstanding achievement in those two years was his ninth place in the U.S. Masters tournament—the best-ever performance in that event by a British player.

NEIL COLES, by retaining the match-play championship at Walton Heath in 1965, set the seal on two years of tremendous success. In 1964 he won nearly £10,000 in prize money, became match-play champion for the first time, and took Palmer to the 35th hole in the final of the Piccadilly World Series at Wentworth after beating the Open Champion, Tony Lema, in an earlier round. At 30 Coles may be said to have more than tasted the sweets of success and can look forward to more helpings.

JIMMY HITCHCOCK, after nearly but not quite making the Ryder Cup team of 1961, entered a lean period and his victory in the Agfa-Gevaert event at Stoke Poges in May 1965 was his first tournament win since 1960, when he became Master Golfer. There is no harder worker then Hitchcock, and his Ryder Cup cap at 34 came as a well-deserved reward for application and dedication.

BERNARD HUNT, with his tall stature and mass of fair wavy hair, has dominated British professional golf for a number of years by the consistency of his performances. 'Big Ben', as his fellow-professionals call him, was a youngster of 23 when he first hit the headlines as a member of the 1953 British team which lost by only one point at Wentworth. He was also in the team which won the Cup at Lindrick in 1957, and in the 1961 encounter he beat the U.S. captain, Jerry Barber. He comes of a family of golfers and his younger brother Geoffrey was in the 1963 Ryder Cup team.

JIMMY MARTIN got his first Ryder Cup place by a run of successes culminating in winning the Piccadilly 72 holes tournament at Wentworth in October 1964—his first major tournament victory. His fortunes in 1965 fluctuated, but he kept adding to his 1964 points to keep his place in the order of merit. He is a true Irishman, capable of great things, and a wonderful putter when in the mood.

CHRISTY O'CONNOR, the laughing Irishman, is so good an iron player that he almost achieves the golfing equivalent of Robin Hood's archery. Coming from the west of Ireland, a fairly inexperienced golfer, to Southport in 1955 he won the first-ever £1,000 prize offered in British golf, and has never looked back. He made the Ryder Cup team in the same year—his first season of British golf—and looks like keeping his place for a long time to come.

LIONEL PLATTS was once regarded as just a big fellow with a big drive. In 1964 he took himself in hand, curbed his exuberant hitting to achieve greater control over direction, and made himself a Ryder Cup player in two seasons. He broke through by winning the Braemar 7-club event in 1964 and achieved a record in the match-play championship of 1965 by winning four extra-hole matches before losing to Neil Coles at the 19th in the final.

DAVID THOMAS has been the enigma of British golf. Possessing all the physical advantages that height, build and strength can confer, he has had to fight lack of judgement in the short game which cost him dear more than once, particularly in past Ryder Cup matches. But he came back to form in the Esso tournament at Moor Park and so confirmed his right to a place in Britain's team.

GEORGE WILL, tall, powerfully built Scot, suffered at one time from an inability to complete the good work, and allowed several tournament chances to slip from his grasp through weak putting in a crisis. But in matchplay he has always been formidable, and when he won the Esso round-robin tournament at Moor Park in 1965 he had definitely 'arrived'.

HARRY WEETMAN's appointment as Captain of the British team surprised many people, but in the weeks of preparation for the match he showed qualities of leadership which augured well for the happiness and efficiency of his side. He had come a long way from 1949 when, as a raw youth who had dabbled in boxing and football before taking to golf, he won the assistants' championship. Then he hit the ball a mile and had no idea of short-game finesse. In no time at all he developed into the complete golfer with rugged strength from the tee and a silky touch on the greens. And so the honours came. In 1953 the only British player ever to beat Sam Snead in the Ryder Cup. Five times a finalist in the match-play championship and twice winner of the title. Twice Master Golfer. And when he took the field with his men at Birkdale it was the eighth time he had faced the Americans in the Ryder Cup.

Captain Weetman and his boys

Captains and friends. Nelson and Weetman before—or
after—the battle

A swing new to British eyes. Dave Marr polishes up his
game before the match

Power and concentration. Arnold Palmer, a winner over
the course, makes even a practice shot look important

British match-play champion Neil Coles lets fly on the
practice ground

'You putt almost as well as Daddy.' Arnold Palmer
practises under the critical eye of Jane, 2½-year-old
daughter of Lancashire professional Tony Coop

Deceptive power. Julius Boros, twice U.S. Open
Champion and oldest member of his team, soon became
a favourite with the crowds

Byron Nelson, forsaking golf shots for snap shots, keeps a
close watch on his men through a 300 mm. lens

Ready to give sterling service. No need to ask why the Mini-Moke score cars were the centre of attention. But these are good drivers of golf balls as well. Former British champion Mrs. Frances Smith on the left, flanked by Miss Susan Ashworth, Miss Gillian Cheetham, Mrs. Joan Rothschild, Miss Pam Tredinnick, Mrs. Ann Booth, Miss Shirley Ward and Mrs. Sheila Irving

Lema lets one go. The 1964 Open Champion winds up
his practice—a characteristic finish to a great swing

'O.K. Let's go.' Ken Venturi, once a Walker Cup
amateur and now a Ryder Cup professional, tries out
his hands after an operation

'That's a long one,' says the spectator as powerful Dave
Thomas puts his beef into a practice drive

Bernard Hunt the stylist finishes strongly and watches
critically as the ball soars over the practice field

That felt all right, Peter Butler seems to be thinking as
he prepares for his first Ryder Cup match

Control and Poise. Christie O'Connor, with a decade of Ryder Cup matches behind him, shows how to keep going

Scot George Will gets into trim for his
second Ryder Cup match

New boy Jimmy Martin from Ireland
works himself into form

Jimmy Hitchcock, Martin's partner against Boros and
Lema, driving in the foursomes

'Champagne' Tony Lema in deep but
out well in the foursomes

Peter Alliss 'splashes' out of sand at
the 14th

Dave Thomas grits his teeth and makes the sand fly against Palmer and Marr

'Well done, partner.' Neil Coles looks on approvingly as Bernard Hunt recovers at the 7th

A movable obstruction. Arnold Palmer (not in the
picture) has driven his ball underneath one of the Senior
Service Mini-Moke score cars. Fortunately these handy
and helpful innovations were extremely mobile

'So that's what we're up against.' Lionel Platts watches as
Tony Lema drives off the second tee in the foursomes

'What do you think, partner?' Billy Casper sizes up a putt on the 14th green while Gene Littler, putter in hand, waits for the verdict

A grandstand view for spectators at the 6th hole as
David Thomas putts, watched by Arnold Palmer, in
the match in which Thomas and Will beat Palmer and
Marr 6 and 5

On the road to revenge. Palmer putts as he and Marr
are on the way to beating Thomas and Will 6 and 5,
completely reversing the morning foursomes result

Twice foursomes winners Alliss and O'Connor congratulate each other

Honours easy. Hunt, Boros, Coles and Lema after halving their foursome

One up on the others. Two of the thousands who saw the matches through periscopes

A loftier view for the TV cameras as Marr, watched by Palmer, prepares to putt on the 14th

A section of 'Arnie's Army' senses the impact of power
as the great Palmer lashes out

Lionel Platts plays a short approach at the second hole

Boros blasts out of a bunker at the 6th

Now it's the turn of partner Tony
Lema at the 14th

Palmer chips at the fourth—

—and partner Marr gets out of trouble

'Oh what a wonderful day!' Bernard Hunt pleases himself—and the crowd—as he holes one to win at the 18th

Casper ready for Coles in the singles
with the Senior Service Press Tower and
Information Board in the background

Thomas, watched by partner Will,
playing from a bunker at the 18th

'That's just great, Billy!' Mrs. Casper makes no secret of her delight as hubby and Gene Littler halve with Platts and Butler

Incredulous Bernard Hunt tells the whole story as a putt fails to go in at the 9th

But the shot came off. Tony Lema, one foot in the
bunker, plays a fine recovery stroke during his brilliant
singles win over O'Connor

It's Casper who's bowed out. Peter Alliss's unusual
acknowledgement as spectators applaud his singles win
over the American

Tommy Jacobs, one of America's new men, finishes a drive

Strength with style. Peter Butler in a characteristic finish

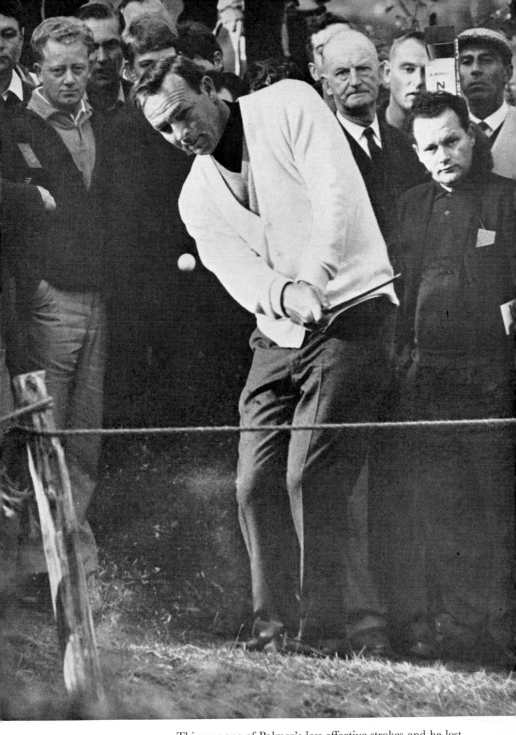

This was one of Palmer's less effective strokes and he lost
the 13th to Jimmy Hitchcock. But not the match

Peter Butler drives in the singles

Lema lines it up

Coming down. George Will unwinding for his opening drive in the singles

Jimmy Hitchcock putts at the 6th against Palmer

A general view of the clubhouse and a typical gallery as
Bernard Hunt finishes the first series of singles

Peter Alliss—power in disguise

Christy O'Connor on the attack

Neil Coles gets out of an
awkward spot

Platts watches admiringly as partner
Butler drives

Neil Coles—always has everything under control

A fine example of Alliss's ironwork

Gene Littler in a tough spot

Dave Marr hits a good one

Thomas putts in the fourball series watched by
partner Will

Bernard Hunt all out

Prime Minister and Past Master.
Mr. Harold Wilson and Henry
Cotton watch one of the singles

Leaders both. Byron Nelson, U.S.
Captain, with Mr. Harold Wilson on
the last day

A precious re-export. The Prime
Minister presents the Ryder Cup to
Byron Nelson

In safe hands. And here it is with the
jubilant winners